PRAISE FOR THE POETRY OF L.

M000086955

For readers and poets alike, Larry Eigner's poems are ▯ ▯ ▯ ▯ ▯ experi-
ence. I have never read anything so particular to the edge of one's own physical body and
the surrounding 'world' in which it lives. Nor have I often met with such lively intellect
and such mastery of poetry's resources. I find him still as impressive and wondrous as I did
those fifty years ago. I was his first publisher, as it happens, and I recall the great excite-
ment and approval given that first collection, *From the Sustaining Air*, by W. C. Williams.
The fact that he had to deal with cerebral palsy as a poet means that his engagement with
and proposal of the given world has always that factor present. Paradoxically, his physical
state proves not a limit of his powers as a poet but, rather, an unexpected sponsor of its
exceptional intellectual and perceptual authority. For me, the importance of his work is
absolute—as would be Robert Duncan's or John Ashbery's or Denise Levertov's or Allen
Ginsberg's. —Robert Creeley

Larry Eigner's oceanic body of work is composed almost entirely of discrete particulars,
available to the senses in ordinary time. By means of an insistent, restless movement, quick
shifts of attention again and again record the harvest of the moment, the manifest, contingent
phenomena of temporal existence. A cosmic ecology in fractal, the truth of the mortality of
the subject is thus built into the apperception of the world at large. "By going around enough
it may be perfect." What more could you ask? —Kit Robinson

Because his physical vocabulary was so finite, Larry Eigner took nothing for granted. Dis-
covering the poem, Eigner took responsibility for every element that showed up on the page,
attaining a thoroughness of control unmatched in the history of English. These stripped down
works have a sculptural—one wants to say "architectural"—logic that can escape a casual
reader. But once you open yourself up to these poems, you will discover yourself entering
one of the great kingdoms of the imagination. —Ron Silliman

Larry Eigner was the first poet to realize the syntactic potential of the page, creating a new
kind of grammar out of the spatial arrangement of words. Other poets relied on conventional
grammar to maintain coherence as their words spread out on the page. Eigner wanted coher-
ence to be discovered as well as maintained, and he found a form for that desire in scatter.
But Eigner's gift only begins in formal innovation. Where it takes him is out, into the world,
perception by perception, word by word, one keystroke at a time. Imagination creating the
universe it inhabits, feelingly. A beautiful, sensation-rich body of work, Eigner's poetry will
arouse your delight and wonder and puzzlement and understanding. An unforgettable expe-
rience of language. —Benjamin Friedlander

Larry Eigner lived intensely in the world and in language, lived in the material, sensual
world intensely through the sensual materiality of language. His poems, at once concisely
focused on the immediate moment yet wide open to its implications, score the movement of
those acts of perception—what he saw and heard and thought and felt—through the cuts and
turns of lineation, the flow and pause of spatial arrangement. It is a remarkable body of work,
and this edition, meticulously edited by Curtis Faville and Robert Grenier, is an extraordi-
nary achievement that presents a full selection of Eigner's poems exactly as he graphed them
on his typewriter. —Albert Gelpi

BOOKS BY LARRY EIGNER

Poems (1941)
From The Sustaining Air (1953)
LOOK AT THE PARK (1958)
ON MY EYES (1960)
THE MUSIC, THE ROOMS (1965)
SIX POEMS (1967)
another time in fragments (1967)
THE- / TOWARDS AUTUMN (1967)
air / the trees (1968)
The breath of once Live Things in the field with Poe (1968)
A LINE THAT MAY BE CUT (1968)
Clouding (1968)
FLAT AND ROUND (1969 and corrected edition 1980)
Farther North (1969)
Valleys / branches (1969)
Circuits—A MICROBOOK (1971)
looks like / nothing / the shadow / through air (1972)
Selected Poems (1972)
words touching / ground under (1972)
WHAT YOU HEAR (1972)
shape / shadow / elements / move (1973)
THINGS STIRRING / TOGETHER / OR FAR AWAY (1974)
ANYTHING / ON ITS SIDE (1974)
suddenly / it gets light / and dark in the street (1975)
MY GOD THE PROVERBIAL (1975 reissued in 2003)
the music variety (1976)
watching / how or why (1977)
THE WORLD AND ITS STREETS, PLACES (1977)
cloud, invisible air (1978)
Flagpole / Riding (1978)
COUNTRY / HARBOR / QUIET / ACT / AROUND—selected prose (1978)
HEAT SIMMERS COLD & (1978)
lined up bulk senses (1979)
time / details / of a tree (1979)
now there's / a morning / hulk of the sky (1981)
earth / birds (1981)
WATERS / PLACES / A TIME (1983)
areas / lights / heights—critical writings (1989)
A Count Of Some Things (1991)
WINDOWS / WALLS / YARD / WAYS (1994)
readiness / enough / depends / on (2000)
The Collected Poems of Larry Eigner (2010)

Calligraphy / Typewriters

The Selected Poems of Larry Eigner

Calligraphy / Typewriters

The Selected Poems of Larry Eigner

Edited by
Curtis Faville and Robert Grenier

The University of Alabama Press
Tuscaloosa

The University of Alabama Press
Tuscaloosa, Alabama 35487-0380
uapress.ua.edu

Publication made possible in part through the generous support of The
Leslie Scalapino – O Books Fund

Inquiries about reproducing material from this work should be addressed to
the University of Alabama Press

Typeface: Times New Roman and Courier

Cover art: Larry Eigner's 1940 Royal manual typewriter;
courtesy of Curtis Faville
Cover design: Curtis Faville and George Mattingly

The editors and publisher wish to gratefully acknowledge Stanford
University Press for permission to republish poems that previously appeared
in *The Collected Poems of Larry Eigner* (2010) and Green Integer for
permission to reproduce poems that previously appeared in *readiness /
enough / depends / on* (2000).

Library of Congress Cataloging-in-Publication Data

Names: Eigner, Larry, 1927–1996, author. | Faville, Curtis, editor. |
Grenier, Robert, editor.
   Title: Calligraphy typewriters : the selected poems of Larry Eigner / edited
by Curtis Faville and Robert B. Grenier.
   Description: Tuscaloosa : The University of Alabama Press, 2016. | Series:
Modern and contemporary poetics | Includes bibliographical references and
index.
   Identifiers: LCCN 2016004837| ISBN 9780817358747 (pbk. : alk. paper) |
ISBN 9780817390549 (e book)
   Classification: LCC PS3509.I47 A6 2016 | DDC 811/.54—dc23
   LC record available at https://lccn.loc.gov/2016004837

CONTENTS

FOREWORD
THE IMAGINED RETURNING:
LARRY EIGNER'S ENDLESS SONG

By Charles Bernstein

Larry Eigner was born in Lynn, Massachusetts, on August 7, 1927, and spent most of his life in nearby Swampscott, midway between Boston and Gloucester, just a few blocks from the ocean. Eigner lived in his parents' house in Swampscott until 1978, when, shortly after his father's death, he moved to Berkeley, where he lived until his death in 1996.

These facts are bare, commensurate to Eigner's poems, which bear witness to the preternatural spareness of his life, just as they bear the weight of a gravitational aesthetic force field unprecedented in American poetry. That's an extravagant claim for a poet who averted extravagance. And it's an incredible claim too, given Eigner's obscurity: despite legions of fervent readers, Eigner's magisterial four-volume, almost 2,000-page *Collected Poems*, received virtually no public recognition when it was published by Stanford University Press in 2010. With this volume, *Collected* editors Robert Grenier and Curtis Faville have created a perfectly scaled introduction to the full scope of Eigner's work.*

To be an obscure poet is not to be obscure, to invert John Ashbery's quip that a famous poet is not famous. Eigner's work has made an indelible impact among the generation of poets brought together in the iconic 1960 *New American Poetry* anthology. Eigner's poetry was recognized early on by Robert Creeley, Charles Olson, Denise Levertov, and Cid Corman and was subsequently published by hundreds of small press editors in pamphlets, books, and magazines. In 1978, Bruce Andrews and I put an essay by Eigner on the cover page of the first issue of *L=A=N=G=U=A=G=E,* and Ron Silliman dedicated his related anthology *In the American Tree* (1986) to Eigner. Robert Grenier, his greatest champion, has placed Eigner's work at the center of an American poetry tradition that begins with Pound and Williams, a view shared by the prescient French poet Claude Royet-Journoud. Grenier writes of Eigner's work (and his own) as "words in space," noting the significance of the visual spacing on the page as distinct from concrete and visual poetry but no less inextricably linked to the technical means of alphabetic reproduction, in this case the manual typewriter. As in the *Collected*, the editors have remained true to the page space and typewriter font that is intrinsic to Eigner's practice. His poetry is, to extend a motto of Olson, *composition by typewriter page.*

Eigner's pages can be seen as etchings on a "blind glass" (to use a phrase of Gertrude Stein's) or opaque windowpane: it is as if the words float in an infra-thin emulsion. As you sit with the poem, letting it slowly emerge, its depth becomes as incalculable as "the sustaining air" Eigner evokes in a February 1953 poem. The play of depth and surface, figure and ground, metaphor and linguistic materiality, thought and image, description and event, and, above all, duration and instantiation is everywhere in these poems.

The poetry of Larry Eigner was profoundly shaped by his cerebral palsy that resulted from a difficult birth. A wheelchair allowed him mobility, but his speech was slurred, and he wrote and typed with just his right index finger and thumb. While Eigner rarely mentions his physical condition in his poems (which mostly involve looking out from, rather than looking onto, himself), the ontology of the poems, the way they lay bare their embodiment, is everywhere informed by the physical circumstance of his being in the world. A worthwhile exercise is to read an Eigner poem with and then without the frame of his disability. This toggling will begin to activate his poetry's 4-D potentiality (the fourth D being duration): the poems follow the modernist principle of imitating not the look but the conditions of nature, and as such they are able to reflect serial projections without being determined by any one of them.

Eigner rarely uses the conventional "I" of lyric poetry; in that sense, his work is an extension of the poetics associated with Mallarmé, Stein, and the Objectivists. Eigner does speak through his poems, just as his gaze, like his awareness, is a constant companion in reading. But these poems are grounded not in the poet's expression but in each reader's perception. As Eigner puts it, the poem is "an / event in your eye" (Oct. 3, 1967) or "on the eyeballs" (Dec. 1–6, 1972). Eigner creates poems that provide active thinking fields for perception (or to reverse that, perceptual fields for reflection). The poems are proof of a daily, meditative practice. For those looking for plot or props or effortless reading, just as for those not looking for those things, this book will push against sensations of entropy, tedium, sameness, emptiness . . . until the features that gave rise to those sensations set off aesthetic endorphins, opening doors to the sublime.

It's a question of scale. A snail's pace is not slow to a worm. Even geologic time has a rhythm.

The particular circumstances of Eigner's worldly life are the ground of his writing. I await Jennifer Bartlett's biography to illuminate the daily life of the poet. Eigner, who stayed in his childhood home much of his life, had a lifestyle that was markedly different from his fellow countercultural New American poets, with their drugs, lovers, and rock 'n' roll. Eigner spoke in a way that was hard for the casual or new listener to comprehend, but he came in loud and clear if you gave him the time. His primary relationship was with his parents and especially his mother, Bessie, who must be acknowledged for supporting her son in a way that heroically defied 1950s norms about his prospects.

Eigner's work offers exemplary realization of an alternative to the sexual politics that lacerates much twentieth-century poetry. He is a key American Jewish poet, though he rarely makes references to specifically Jewish subjects ("my mother is Jewish," he writes on June 9, 1976, "she thinks so"). Eigner grapples with a poetics (and immanence) of the ordinary that connects him to Stein, Louis Zukofsky, Charles Reznikoff,

George Oppen, Jackson Mac Low, Hannah Weiner, and Ted Greenwald. In this respect, I think also of Lorine Niedecker, James Schuyler, Ron Silliman, Lyn Hejinian, and Grenier. Eigner seems to be evoking William Carlos Williams's "Between Walls" when he writes, "between walls the light / to give / blankness in shadow" (January 1961). I read these lines as an ars poetica: the play of light and shadow creating the animated blankness of the page. Is this a literary allusion or is it a Zen koan? I think of Philip Whalen (to whom Eigner dedicates a poem), Norman Fischer, Leslie Scalapino, John Cage. You don't need these overlays to appreciate Eigner but after a while, you get to play. For example, Dickinson's "You cannot solder an Abyss / With Air" and Blake's doors of perception both come to mind with Eigner's "refresh the eyes / against the abyss" (October 1959); note, not *your* eyes or *my* eyes. "Refresh" brings to mind blinking, a serial scanning akin to moving frames of film. Each moment anew.

Eigner's sudden paratactic leaps / syntactic-synaptic jump cuts—the basic prosodic movement of his poems—are electrifying. Following Dominique Fourcade, I think of Manet's motto "Tout arrive"—everything happens in the blank space of the page. In place of the poem as a record of psychodrama beyond the poem, action in Eigner arrives at the level of the phrasal hinge: a reinsistent prosody of shift / displacement / reconstellation. *Textual slivers shimmer.* The poet drops away as the world keeps arriving: a be-in of the beginnings of middleness (in medias res).

A leap of faith, *this* to *that*: "suddenly / . . . / (to leap / and break" (1955 #j7). Eigner's radical ordinary averts symbols and confessions. The intensifying movement of fragments-in/as-appositions, Eigner's algebra of connection-in/as-inflection, is never abstract or dissociated: poetic feet land on the perceptually concrete.

These poems sublime the sublime.

Only this and nothing more.

```
The imagined, returning
     what is
               endless song (June 19, 1970)
```

—Provincetown, Massachusetts
August 7, 2014

NOTE

* Eigner also wrote essays, which have been collected as *Areas Lights Heights: Writings 1954–1989*, ed. Ben Friedlander (New York: Roof Books, 1989). Additional material online at the Electronic Poetry Center (epc.buffalo.edu/authors/eigner), including biographical notes by Grenier and Friedlander and an autobiographical compilation by his brother Richard Eigner. Recordings of Eigner reading and talking, including an interview with his friend Jack Foley, are available online at the Eigner PennSound website (writing.upenn.edu/pennsound/x/Eigner.html).

A NOTE ON THE TEXT

In 2010, Stanford University Press published *The Collected Poems of Larry Eigner*, in four volumes, containing over 3,070 poems (the source text for this book). In the course of editing that earlier, comprehensive work over a seven-year period, the present editors realized that, given the vast body of the *Collected*, a selected poems was needed to concentrate and focus Eigner's life's work, so that many of the best poems could be held in the hands, and *experienced*, in one book.

Calligraphy / Typewriters is divided into two sections—Swampscott / 1945–1978, and Berkeley / 1978–1995—so that the work may be presented as conceived, environmentally located, and understood by Eigner in his life experience (primarily in his parents' house at 23 Bates Road, Swampscott, Massachusetts until his father's death in 1978 and subsequently 'on his own' in a house with friends and providers in Berkeley, California).

Typographically (as was the case with the *Collected Poems*)—since we agree with Eigner that his typewritten text (accomplished with right index finger and thumb, working on his 1940 Royal portable typewriter) creates a kind of 'typewriter calligraphy'[i]—we have replicated the typewriter's equivalent spacing, to reproduce and preserve Eigner's meticulous vertical and horizontal settings of letters, words and lines of varying lengths and shifting (potential) positions on the space of a page.

Chronology has been preserved whenever possible (though sometimes compromised in the interest of saving space—and paper, as Larry liked to do, by putting multiple poems on one page to have them be more available to him with his one useable hand), so that a reader might read Eigner's life work (in 'short form') as a single unified arc, from near its beginnings to its end.

A short section of Notes (gathered from the *Collected*) is appended, to provide some information about certain poems.

We gratefully acknowledge the encouragement and assistance of Charles Bernstein and Hank Lazer, and that of our editor, Dan Waterman, at the University of Alabama Press—as well as the support and help of Richard Eigner, Larry's surviving brother—without whom this edition would never have been.

Curtis Faville
Robert Grenier

---

[i] Our title (*Calligraphy / Typewriters*) owes its origin to the following marginal note by Larry Eigner, on the original typescript of his poem No. 1117, dated January 3, 1979: "First 2 lines might be / a good title for a Col / lected Poems" (*see* poem on p. 263 below).

SWAMPSCOTT

1945-1978

Sonnet

Sometimes, at night, when I can hear the ocean,
After a hot and sultry summer's day,
It sweeps me with a smooth and mighty motion
Into a land of dreams, a phantom bay.
And landing there, I stand upon the beach.
Looking about me, I can see a light
On the horizon: far beyond my reach,
A star is falling towards it in the night.
The air is moistened by a drop of rain.
Here are no burning suns, no hot sands baking.
Within the confines of my little brain,
There seems to be a world of my own making.
I see a million stars and in my hand
I sift a thousand grains of moonlit sand.

c. 1952

I
I can only play one note at a time
(and I've got ten fingers) This is the piano

and I should think of something I have to

        play
and have to vary   without looking

    from   precision of simple things

  bam

        with only that and
        the tune in my mind

"Keep at it," they say when they see L.
reading, then disappear down the front steps
 and plenty die, playing the black market
  a heart attack in middle age

        in the blackout
waiting for death, wanting sleep
and the walls had nothing more to reflect

      world
            the sea
a shock wave
 and fliers a mile away
were planes of another country

Afterwards the sun came around

and they say how
stars will collide

                    B

Is it serious, or funny?
Merely?

          Miasma of art
                          The

more the merrier is my view

seeing the levels of the world

and how easily emptied space

                              is

Here they made the perfect pots
on the beastly floors
the spoons and knives randomly dealt

and tread on the pine-cones
bare-footed
to cut wood

and here,the women went undone
till noon, plaiting

 Once this happened
and the cooks brought food to their seniors in wigs
in dressed-stone mansions;

I am omnipresent to some extent,
but how should I direct my attention

sufficiently to what I desire, to
stop, to
what is charging on the roadbed, what
          going away, the
fire-gong, people and busses

     and even in my room, as
I know
            the waving sun
                          the

constant ephemerals

The midnight birds remind me of day
though they are
                    out in the night
beyond the curtain I can't see

Somehow bedrooms don't carry
tradition I
and the boxed radio
is off. But what am I reading

inward performance

Has relevance. Allows me to hear
while something speaks. As for the bed
straightened by visible hands
only is it huge
when I feel down in darkness

          D y i n g

And yet they hunt the great whales
    the beauties they see
finally dwarfing them

Around the world
                What's more
they name them, and these are not tags
but inexpressibles

their function

and even the unwanted,

and time

to think lower than
                    spheres

N o i s e   G r i m a c e d

Noise grimaced
we took pleasure in the heavens
    the close sky
although we knew we could not have seen it
and the flash fell expanding the light
up the beds and walls at once
dying, leaving the star distant
although we had known all season's heat
      like a room's still air here

slowly I have sometimes heard my ears click
as if some naked siftings bared themselves
and who know how these needles come to the body

Another moment Day passing or

beside it,
          out of the corners of the eyes
   the wind like the rain, it can't be swallowed
rain as rain, walls shut in
virtue of walls, Rain is a forest
but the wind is too light for a sea
   Under it still the skin is unquenched

And there are not two dangers either
none moving away, in front forwards
  to my head

though sometime it will rain, hail or
                          still more variety
gripping the shoulders
                    before or after our deaths

                    O   p   e   n

They nod at me and I at stems
Yes, I agree But I flower myself.
or can't change

Yes, passes.   As I,pass on the air
As i,   pause
As i dream, sight
 I have been on all sides
        my face and my back

Disappears   any time   a world   can
Reality   dissolve

        abstract, abstract, O little
                        seeing that word
blue against the stack-
            o i walk i walk

the pavements
assume they are yellow

        the flowers seem to nod

February 53

from the sustaining air

fresh air

There is the clarity of shore
And shadow, mostly, brilliance

summer
        the billows of August

When, wandering, I look from my page

I say nothing

   when asked

I am, finally, an incompetent, after all

E n v i r o n s

Many shapes of wings
on the sky and the table;
and large men carefully at dusk
lengthened by lights   watering their lawns

turn, paterfamilias

   and the sweet hay as I go
   from one foot to the other
 more so than I might
 mingled with barber's tonic
 from the morning's shops
   of papers and bright rag
            as if we could
            take time out for life

  and the afternoon's seas,   like yards

At some smell of smoke
I found a spray behind me
and the two on my right gone
  tending the grass, all night
 everyone beautifully
   (by themselves   the same thing

 time   for the surroundings

        against the strip of hill
        ending low, a space
        on this side, hut for clouds

the dark swimmers
 their heads in the sun

       If time shd stand still
you can't see it move

which way does the river go
 partially the

 wind,   and light,   Down waves
        the indefinite flooring

the toppled clouds
the squared mountain

I have felt it as they've said
   there is nothing to say

there is everything to speak of
  but the words are words

when you speak that is a sound
What have you done, when you have spoken

  of nothing
  or something I will remember

After trying my animal noise
i break out with a man's cry

The fountain of youth is a poetry
and whether we are one minute older
the present always arrives

come as we make it
According to our healths
(when we are sitting still)

but time itself kills

the brush, consumed or not
                    and the individual
which is needed) dies

                    necessities dying out

but nothing ends
as everything begins

        Near the beginning

she fed him peanuts in the zoo
which quieted

surrounded by a civilization
the bear and the odd monkey

        pawed
     at nothing
                the fleas in the meshed air
                their suitable hides

        and the visible flies

     the monkey businesslike
     the peacock unsurprised

            and earth
        the dirt was simple

the keeper at meals
retreated to dark huts

        holding his hand near a cage

        he supported the sun
        it had rained some days before

        and the sunset was cloudy   11

IT SOUNDED

and tangled dry-

        like fire
     at the start of the day
       the engines
            control
but the wind in the twigs
or thistles, stalk

     the birds are violent
     the spring

they function by shouting

suddenly

all day

the houses stand some paint in
glass the dusty sun

with the fresh air

and the man who fixes the roof

top and

the transformer below

nothing except the wires
and the trees

     and the boys climbing
            the shed
       (to leap
       and break

so what if mankind dies?

                    the birds
     the croak and whistle
     has no future, either

so what?
so what?

the future arrives

the end of a stick
in my crotch

toward the speed of light

                    S t e p - w i s e

The sea dances the heavy lights
below the wall; a distant
crash sinking,   matched changes of color

strain and confusion, out of which the storms are bred up
after this hour, hunting for sewage and spells
garages and the back yards
where the arrowheads might sift behind the woods

              hammering wings   the
              hutch   the
              boat lifting between houses

   there is the screening of loam,to
   leave the rocks out, pitiful ash
   crumb in the dropless afternoon
   of wine-cellars, accents
   of ancient yeasts   and that wire
   slant of sky filling our eyes
           blind, to run back
   the beaten snatches of dust through the rain
              or violent cold   echo

   They hunt clams In a lull
   at the sewer outflow we dribble our own banks

                   dwarfing tin
              and blocked sand whistles, gouge
                quaking
                   pebbles floated in the night like ghosts

bird-speckled, The wall reins
the barren grains of sand, bareness of shadow
the mud levels endlessly stilled

           awnings endowed serene

   Then later
           to return and
   pop balls on the empty brick
     and mortar, (the dirt stirs, the sparrows on the
         nest overhead in the drain split jaws
      as the sunset, in full, passes down

children's sizes are indeterminate

then there's those ones across the road
they live from a lawn split by a driveway

--well, let's go in, the kitchen someplace in the middle
the tv in the corner down the aisle ,
the basement window shows the circled grass

the kids have a dog that's ownership
Where he keeps his hat, they sometimes put on
they push the sidewalk for four lots
and
            take a diaper car for a milktruck

so a year is a long time
the snow more reflective than the glass
they see coming at moments in their minds
  and far away,the trees stay bare

in the fall the cats will spawn, usually
and birds come out in the sky, the nests dry
like crusts, and plants in the earth, fires at the gutter
the hens smelling the chickencoop
or garages hot, ragged water and oils
they rake up the beds with their toys

D a y s

Just like when she was little
the cricket sang, but the
sky was remote
this summer
        the hen-yards obsolescent
and the walls often not very wide
the bed a ship to sail again
yet more of a ring, dissolving in the waves

she tossed from side to side, there was
nothing under her, there was nothing
under her, to feel, she had gone too far away
 .bed,and a quiet night

The clouds went over, the trees grew
                                          out
covered, different from weeds softly off earth in the
non-violent sun

     broken)

                              wires stay on
                         carrying messages
                   of no content, but   steady

the birds roost

                    she had moved a moment
                 the 13th floor
              the room all fixed
              up the stairs
              to the roof the
                grating
                 old heat
                                        outside
                                         the walls

                         smokes, matches simultaneous with
                         idea
                                                 change

                    the cellar, all at one time the
                    room

               phone by the window

               to do anything
               across the country

          voyages
             somewhere near the beginning

the rain noses in front of your face
when the clouds thicken, the vague increase

        gives you a silence

                though widest are the blue points
        of the ultimate reach, taking itself

                to the sides   wherever you go

            below which the hammer-thin clouds
            beach their imperceptible ways

she lies at the world

in thought, as before

    looking up again, without need of a bed

                or thinking, where there used to be hens

        fallen asleep

                                        c. 1957   # x 8

Night. Everything falls flat
The dump of the world. Even within gravity,
the cold. There is a woman
 playing piano   we do not see color
for some space   There were green trees, the country,

  The houses were farminghouses. The phonograph, too
        simple as a road. The ceiling is white
And somewhere now clouds leave the sky

   Look at it, the keyboard's marking time
   inside like a harp something
   breakable, it's as if eternal

   the thing drags out, had to be figured out
   a long time back   she remembers the tones

   in FRance. There will be some years after this
   after last year

                    she wears glasses
    at least in giving a study, patience

        echoes   leaves, distantly
          blocking the window
                        in the broad dark

        at the muffed room   17

BRINK

    the less I
    take for granted

      the world going forward

         I am getting
         no younger

       an illusion of this
          no, a

        death

announced
         Sometimes a squirrel

      affectionate dogs
      nosing in spring
      off the corners

          cars, carts
      on final levels
      stretched up

              and the overhead craft
              in all weather
              like windows

          Whales
     conduct a feast
     near the cold used surface
     awave like floes
        the broken-off scraps
           smells

        the huge climate

             o a lively day
          keen
            light, imperceptible turn

        coffin of justice
            among bottles and fruit

     the beach I hear not quite
     the next road
               dancing

       pavement of threads, things
       horns bicycles   papers
       on hands

because the street-light shines
steady
and the leaves fall
like a few stars
throughout the night

and the trees moving their bones
in the wind
which doesn't need light

the cold wind Lethe

the strong wind they sleep

the objects of a dream

growing

letting their
hands, such as they have, down

they are unconscious of
the sun

A response

the muffled trees

  Later it snows
that is, after the
leaves and the sun

     Considerable time
variety of paths

through the same space, thickens
and piles up

what was maybe fog
when the sea smelt

and came back

as it comes back

now

the tides

          the sun spinning
          the moon having its
          different sides
          the world
          hardening

             the trees pore
             white under the shadows,
             the fading, loose sea

          G r o u n d

today the rubbish truck
        has a green body

it is autumn here the leaves still on the trees

early,   though distant morning, forenoon sun,
                immediate struggle, bent
            card, cans, boxes,
dusts, a toy
shovel, a bottle, assorted pages,
wrapping, socks, the iron to a mattress
                but no bone
                or, since the war, cat-scraps

        there was once a hound burying one
        until he placed the right barrel

smoky straw stamped out in the wind
packing   parked minute

on minute
            as far as I can remember
it has always been full, the eventual stations
progress
when it's about to rain

        the green slats again
today put up like a wall, filling
the gap in one side

            garbage long, low and slant-roofed

            and the ice-cream goat that reputedly ate tin
            perhaps in Bolivia
            a clean pediment behind

and they all used to dump out back of my house

                the loads piled high
moved in the wind
        they stick
heaved up over the shoulder,
        like hay in a nest, stomped
down, ashes, that barked music,
                        however

apotheosis

        idle from
        the teeming field

            pin buttons
            the queer shine in the weather
            to rust

```
        The river of waste
    swiftly, the rain speeds
        and slows up

not like when I was a boy, change-over,

        the earliness
        as tomorrow
        and the next day
```

```
                                    c. 1957    # y 4
```

```
D o   i t   y r s e l f
```

```
Now they have two cars to clean
the front and back lawns
bloom in the drought

                    why not turn the other radio on the
        pious hopes of the Red Sox

  yes, that's a real gangling kid coming down the street

  he'll grow up

            he'll fill out

        sponges with handles

            we got trinaural hearing

    -they are taller than their cars
```

The Breath of once Live Things

In the field with Poe

                    yes, Wolfe
this harvest, harbor of stars
the up-turned mirror in the window
earth   on my bureau

        the blank face

                        pale and tremendous
        dawn, blinding
        eyes over the sun

    sodden and unfamiliar
    the hours change
            to the south

    a man's proper stature
                            project

        I've been a bad boy

    no personal god,because
    we couldn't settle down

            too big to
        ride rails

                    freight

        it's true, at the heavy back, all of us, those
        tapestries are light

      your face forming
                    too great a height
            into a grave

            a hole in the lawn
        or the brick steps

    robins may eat worms
      or fallen leaves
                    the suns

            work

        to have a good
        time

        all
                together
    a baby comes fictitiously
        into the world
    he seizes as concrete
    Milestones the caterpillar's

inch
unable ever to gauge

        butterflies

  and the thrashings of man
  making the seasons heavy

                  the moon thin
                      as may be

          bees

they sleep

        bows of the spring

again

      fish
near a rough tank

  steep
      inland

  behind waves

 the piers splintering
 simple pieces of light

       That lump of a moon, in the sky
       past like anything you want
       complete
         all seen with different eyes

   fading off slowly, halves

   by halves

       divided windows
  bring in the shattering depths

then clouds

I think what passes over our heads
are the huge things

       lightning, blind

split

  naked immensities of the whole

        the stroke of it
      bars over the street
      and poles no higher than the leaves
         branches

        time intact of the body   **23**

        invisible extent

Leaving myself, I leave eternity
God, Melville said, nearly to begin
yet the moments are undivided; window-frames are objects
occupying nothing
but plain space

          streamlined? hardly, you'd say
except in parts
and a little odd, too, and
            always both sexes way
inside, millions of islands, as
rough an element as we've got,   but
                Wind, there are other things
like stripping and handling parts
as we find them, propping them there
to be more attractive why
that fish, driven all over
by it like a storm   by which she sailed
enough staging
to float on, but not with their wives

          a fine business, even so

              whatever size you please

That island, too, spread one white eye
which we give it
if we can

                  (caveat

  the parts relating to each other
not even the absolute

The sky was empty, right above my head
    emptiest of all, above the gutter
when the gulls passed on
          with no particular smells
and the leaves held to the puddle
reflecting the wall thin window
                          the new house
  like a junction, complex craft, tenting
the train railing off
          where the sun blazed on the stainless door
          for a couple of hours
  below which I couldn't see
I couldn't walk far enough

    to stand over it

  those leaves about the first to come down

      Identify the earth with consciousness

              they were lost

              standing

              for some time, time

                        all those points to the compass
                the weather arrived

                by such a manner
                        painting on over the sun

        the landscape brought home by sound
        noise

        the jet spines spread in the sky
                        there
        is the waste tractless?

                of outline no possible
        but somehow it's hard

                                circular   that's
                        event
        but the permanent gets more commonplace

                quick

        moments pulling what memory

                                        1958   # 8 c

all these long cars
legal on the black roads
a more certain speed

here's mercury again

a mile of stone   houses ,

 the sea screens the beach

leaves at the top
                hill trees

        birds flock

                we'll never remain
                        by the coal lighthouse

 Let's take to our boats
 and crickets' shoes

                        all kinds
                        protuberating

                        snaky

                                                25

                        series

clouds complicated as stars
high   in the air

  like mountains,   one in the middle

            the
        evening, because of the sun

      above the swimmers, the beach
    men

            those free relations

        mirror the moon in the west

                  ah, those bird-watchers
        have a new object

                Boston

                    hills

          the sign of the earth
          after a rain

            colors November

                the road curved

                  the road straightened
                  that coast lifted off

          another brief shower
          the earth seas

                  sound

              history is tall

              clouds   the lost space

              clouds, the moving doors

        the wind breaks on the corner

        the day in the house

The old papers
        in the old mailbox
                before they're delivered
                  the old houses
     are all right

the grahndstahnd at
  Wonderlahnd

pilate's daughter

      we go again around the pylon

the splendid fuel
tank up

   inquisitive dog
             a jumping boy

    flat on the wind
             ok

   the baby's soon grown

    tenement slice

  the railroad bridge is

  who would think of coating it

 the radio billboard

  which is an ad

   same as the street

as if blindness, the sun
   sudden back of the house, every day

   the moment the world gets so strange

      leaves distantly blocking the window
       in

         cars behind them
         creep under them

       parade   memorial
                  up against the hill

after the drilling continues
   air dance on the street

                                    August 59   # 5 d

   GETTING OLD

            poems about
fences and vines

      on earth, while the sky
holds the quiet
fantastic dimensions
  masses and bits
through which the sun might glare
               the attempt at standing still
   to show nothing is worth
   the final deliberations

the motors and
       islands
                  scattered to infinity

we had a thunderstorm here yesterday and
today's expected again

            pleasant

In August the leaves turn out
to a slow wind

THE WANDERING MOSQUITO

into my face
among the masses

When does he go to sleep
I forget he's irregular

Is there any sleep,at all,for him,
before death?

 he wanders miles and miles and
 becomes aware of the window
 where the moon is

 in a short time

 the peg-board

                and it's raining outside

  94 humid

         he hasn't hurt me yet

    I have to open the window

        his head is a constant drop of blood

illuminated birds
            the persian dark
 ness   in the light of
  middle ages   Insight is
         walking back and forth

     ah, now, the couplings
                        scuffles
      the imagination

   WHERE are the
     five french hens

     O pioneer

                down the street in the sunlight
                    in the sunlight,   the back seats

                    it always looks like new

                the moment was strange

                        the bare shot branches

                the flat-jacketed boys

                    the sun   cloud changes
                    hydrant sides
                            wearing their knees

                    in the cold,
                            not their houses   glassy

                doored flames

                    down to the ground

                                nourishing dogs

                    rough

                    a local cloud strays out

                    freshened   the hill without snow
                    a slant way from night,   on

                    those branches where the roofs twist

                    leaves burrowing distance

memory of sound
instantaneous

      patch of landscape

 how can your little finger
bring up dirt

        ingots

  hunger

the sparrows there for the gulls

  the sea out on its plain

 the sun crosses my view

1959   # 8 h

horse
   hours with his navel
     funny thing
          how
 we return to the sky
      or earth

   wings

```
Plenty of time
        but I can't sleep nights
Life is static after all
 nothing before a man but a woman

                the kaleidoscope of
                sheep on a stone wall

            the mails are unimportant
                    the poles
                running through infinity

            rain spindle the sun

    they hop  keep your eyes on
                            them
                                    they
                form themselves into waves
                        numbers
                            and disappear

                They were going nowhere
                but it takes time

        no good,now    to find
        the heart beat


        suddenly the window seems washed
          the newspapers falling in the
                        opposite bathroom

            I'm right in the reflection

                permanent
                        radio ads

            the clarity  distant from gravel
                the meadow dying
```

The paradox of
the invisible
 once visible

      my painful
    mystery

heading out

  the sun

 rayon

        not here moving, but bent

          a river
          with ducks   curves
           and floats

      welcome that
      appearance

          the whole is divided as you look
            and know well enough

            gleaming in front of the black

                bound to imagine

    how

        in sleep it is no strain

                    poems
                       of the subdued trees

            the huge depths
            may be easy death
            soundless no doubt

      shaken by morning light

      easily

          to enhance itself

              with afternoon
                          stars
               and sea air

                 Water of the flat hood

             night on the moon

the snarl of rain cars
   the people are trivial
and try to go back and forth

      to treat each other

      sit with the windshield wipers

      with all the lightning

    while the rain brings close its summer smell
    boundless over the trees

  gulls raising their wings up through it
    bulb of their furling cry

      How many times,   death
      has cried
      wolf   the

      cloud
       larger than the bay

      the ceiling disappears

      the music
      in air

         the bows, trumpets
               moved

       and the red sunset
      out
       by the window

LETTER FOR DUNCAN

just because I forget
to perch different ways
                the fish
     go monotonous

               the
     sodden hulks of the trees
     in a glorious summer

you don't realize
 how mature you get
        at 21

     but you look back

        wherever a summer
           continue 70 seasons

           this one
             has been so various

             was the spring hot?

  every habit

    to read

 nothing you've done you have

        older

           the fish
     can't bother screaming

        flap by hook

        the working pain

               jaws by trying a head   bodies

        you'll always go to sleep
         more times than you'll wake

                    g a b l e

The sun and stars
part of the world
a rain
        glazed roof
    you look out

   clouds
  about the shape of yesterday
          insubstantial

              coast
            aisle
          even after snow, in the cold

                        where you find them

                              any animal
                              grown roots

          the
              sky   exchange of its lids
              evening bald
                    plungers

baying
depths of the land
submerged

a queer
          underground
    surfacing

   towards dead inchoate
          fish   damp   snake

        reeds climb
              slope

        swum by   an illusion of a waterfall

            borne in

            to the country grains

          the wave crag
        permeated life
            slamming up

        the imagination
      is in the mouth
              oceans
                  tide

```
        unceasing   continual
    pitches   hospitals
    the eye   sweeps


            far out

how much of the earth
```


                                                    1959   # 6 k


```
        wings fluttering up near the
        beginning of rain

  I like to see
the pink car wet
wheels   matched by a pool

                the rain
                  muddy in sound

  imagine it tipped
    besides what it is both
        semicircles

            steep the gutter

      the light water
        as much as you look to see
            houses which are the same

                double   barrel

        the passion for cars     gone

        the present as quick as showers
                and the past
                        fallen

            a rainbow maybe
        somewhat behind trees

            enough years
```

g u t t e r

toe bigger tonight
dependent on
how you put it

the room being an old one
now

these rooms,   and their clothes
closets

reeling, winter, fish on the
porch

end clouding to get wet
shelves

The clock's moving
at a nice speed

in the circle of things

the amplifier, silence

embrace of two flies
on my knuckle
the wings rattling
ears

it isn't the season

the radio
cans

the musty-
lighted world
in the afternoon

trees   the wind
touched by cloud

field ,   in the same space

summer, again
ordinary

it will have to sicken

                    a thing about
              a plane pulling a sling
                    letters   but how did I
                    get it down

                              on paper

              below the public
                 prints on wheels
                 they deliver the good
                          which smells

                 and the miles lie quiet

              you can't lower an equation without
          resort to zero

                 What's past?
                              Let the runway
                    stop here   the old corn grows
                    invisible mostly

                                   remote

                    in the sound of people
                       bathing by a lake

                              clouds

        Emptiness, house, the wind
    a mere buffer in the trees
       not just a sound,   exercise stripped
             for another
           seasonal attempt the clouds have moved off
       the sky is blue   ravines
       alter behind the branches this is what they have been waiting
    for
          unconsciously
                          it is lasting all day
                                         What
          are birds for?
                       rivers
          to the crotches cliffs

                 ocean drops turbulent the dying
                    leaves, the street   which
                    one night, will escape ridden

                    cover the seeds, how
          can they take on
                 the broad dance,

                                                    39

                 the numb bark, wild,
                    the wind streams on

```
These are the
winners  of the game  motorcycles
            him ahead she looking
                            behind
                        the wind in lids
      a town    clouds clear under
                    fresh morning
            a ride through noon    transmute forever


      the seasoned old dr.
        who exuded the hard  human
      breath  legacy of latin
    from the chair    usual organs  the brief
        wounds of the still young  out on the field
            in a slouch


          the season of winners and
            everyday    hoo-ray for
r i b b o n e d   school    lean out the windows to
b e a c h w a g o n pound,  as long as you pass
      i v o r y
    s h o c k e d   c a r s          the indians, coming
                            going with
                    the secret clearings of


        moments that are hidden
          by trees, ramifications
          deepening leaves when they
        beat the bleachers at the
          ultimate reading
                            ravines


        felt downward by the squirrel


                saturday
          the concentration of spectators
          blowing their horns, nose, to extend
        the band or something, beyond the
      ninth choral wave
        they made, though the band, at the same time
        drums out, like the soldiers they are
      like


          the siren air raid test
          topping if off, become
        a feature    doom saturdays  an
          open city


          as the young scatter


        and horns again  some reason  near
                                sunset
```

          the far bliss   home
           in the risen sun,   the country

    the stream like a serpent, or fish

                       to go down

           the harbor teeming
           with broad flats   but then

           the horizon

                    trailing back

     the merrygoround in the park
     away from the slips

       the horn goes off to the piccolo

               the thunder mists

           moving up a course

             F a c e

               under
               him

           the bed
              the table
           a chair
              through

                crawling
                           flight

             around

                flat

             crowded

             safe

                working

the rain
 rank draping   bale
   radios of the world even the
     tall buildings from a distance   under our
   dust covers capacitors

       along stone the
     industry   cloudy roofs
       with washline days balls
     have peaked the 4th floor and
     accelerated   the negative

       furnitures   sections of the sidewalk
         the shorefront a few
         streets over   arias
         cathedral a separate pocket
     actually, in the other direction
       ,towering
       arches with trees, ivy

     to the middle of
       country boughs, ;the wind
   wades   and the rain
         down importunate as a
           cat

         hanging out magnificent
       coal slides and sooty
         arms of the burners   drams
             chipped rims of the basement wells

     steaming to the jungle
   erect brassed through the bedrooms and
     office labelled panes   as the

       water flushes down behind a
         dentist ranged with the
           sheriff   the

     public staircase   insurance
       behind doors   standing
             open in hot weather   inside
       where a cat emerges
     who scrabbled the windows mineral
         water the
         sort of escalator he, suddenly
         is, beyond the
         narrows geranium grill

             like the
         trellis we've platted out
       woodwards   advancing the
       old orchard view   the mind

         not refinable
       from the kitchen   where
           faggots are not housed

```
           splinters in the rain
       or high sun


   that sound,
           a real autumn in gusts

       to dispose of summer
                       leaves




                                   October 59    # 3 m


       t o  C  C


   how read it
           line after line

                        given
               one look

                   refresh the eyes
               against the abyss




                                   November 59    # 1 m


   blast    blueness mouth with the sky

       time spread  the mind

                           car

       clouds  raised as if
           mute     passed
       away from the room in houses and

                       the child

               long sun    as it

       shows the sea also

               the branches fewer now

       slowly forgotten  for a

               rising again    rustle

               color of trees

   wind brief courses                            43
```

the discursive how
        packed
    lives

        and by the echo

        dissolved

                        as the
                forcing together

    a pile of screens
                        you could leave acquire
                time,   flies
                        reverberating

        the dark house, and the vast
                sun moving, out,
            slowness, level of it all

                approach night

            the clouds to the sea

                stirred   on

Again dawn

        the sky   dropped
                its invisible whiteness

                we saw   pass out
                            nowhere

                    empty the blue

                        stars

            our summer
                        on the ground

            like last night another
                                    time

in fragments

       I s l a n d s

            My backyard the stars that
            wind should be hard at the corner
      nightly the lavish bed
      taking me nowhere   how

   I grew up thinking with time
   that doesn't   the sky
   deserted, dark, made the oceans
   cold,   the sand
   damp, hard   many dawns have flushed up

     and the coast has a road   at the
     houses   turned over boats
     which may be narrower than
     when they ride out in the bay
     and further still into
          the quiet, nearly equal
               on both sides   the nets

       and the shaded map of the cliff

       elsewhere
                 beginning to sleep

            the cricket drills
            constant in the field

         past self
                   and the present
      window with
        a back yard
                      life on the wall

                 birds
         flight
         doubling,
                   pecks at the barrels
            after the dog like shadows

            I
      step to a western saloon
        with some nice glass

sleepless a week but
    windy last night

nothing to do

with the arms wrestling
    trees reel

            to block the whistle

   The shine was on the beech
     and the sun is beyond in the sky

      A n   I m i t a t i o n

           (a shot of Rbt Creeley)

What has that face got to do with that
 poetry? In

   order to have one you need the other, yes

            the sky
   would do as well   I know
Questions are funny, a flower

   of life then Let's
go on   What are the leaves
     in back What's
   the sky doing in your head? The

 photos of some of your
"predecessors" What

 has your voice to do with
the thoughts which at least pass
in my own life, its

   hurry
         While the churches
are open as the earth   There are statues

   in all the museums and
around them now in the park and

      even in the wilds
         again

      and paintings of stars, nights,
    in walls
            opposite mirrors

46

S h a f t s

        a wind
hardly
     to listen to

denotes a river

     play on

          footsteps

        material
          gapping

        woods cloud over
          white in the sky

      sunny decembers also
          and the close months
                            cliffs

            stony perhaps
          in the bay

      where life too is a wall

    there will be ice, and melt

      even in descent, or

        of course re-frame

        the gutters dirty with grit

    where the girls took any direction

        lodged fins or eyes

        actually feathers   heads maybe

        or arrows

              slopes   room for all

                particles
                        outlines

A glass
  of water

   complexate
     waves

outdoors
  broken

 bottom   pitch   all that left
        of vacuous sand

   and cut off   a sharpened

     edged core   crawling there
                              things

        the uneven section

             sun

          baked

           cold underground

          water is everywhere
           enough to be solid

              where a tuft even

           hangs in it   and then the deep vessels

             ride   sea sprouts   there
               is a table

            broken
                    into

before dying
        crosses his toes
                at will

    or then in the morning again

            the sun up

        slowly

            it wasn't the time

        and the unspeakable leaves
                    remaining

    slowly is the way

            time   absolute

        you speed up

    it does not dissolve

            the stomach takes
            the punishment

                    or it's durable

        small bones in the head

            a death
            to memory

concrete

　　like those bad heads
　　children have

　　　　idea
　　of the connection

　　funny

　　　if you stand
　　　　under

　　　voices

　　　　one end is at the right

　　　　　and piles
　　　been through a screen
　　　　　　starting sounds

　　　/
　　　　　familiar tides
　　　　　　　　　single shores
　　　　　towards night

　　and steady cold   animals

　　　　　　　get through the woods

　　　　　　relaxed heads

　　　　　individual

　　　　old man

　　　dream echoes

　　some increase   the vibration

　　　looked into by flies

the knowledge of death, and now
 knowledge of the stars

        there is one end
                        and the endless

    Room at the center

     passage /in no time

    a rail   thickets hills   grass

blades of grass
under the miles
            along air

        the missile
                is a failure

                birds rush
        and their thirst like water

human
humus

  said the arci
        geo anthrr

      in his large suit

      mostly it's comic

        tomb burial

      you know, what is
            identify

      or else distinguished

    reference   "this gentleman

    by the flap of the hut

        in this sketch where
            there was a woman too

              mail-house dress

            all the bones are white

          delicate paddling of pots

          all over way to europe

        yes but the actions
            larger than words
                    the language

            might have survived

      notches for the thrower

        very valuable   of course the

          beasts they slaughtered

              behind

      "hunters, like glorified animals

    puzzle our skulle

        in towns they met people every day

          there's a polish. stone
                    to look in

idyl
ideal
    wood
 and the outboards

        leaving you empty
                fall to sleep

        still children   next day

    always plenty to
    dream

  the bouncing spray

        the walls are
        loose really

    your hands
    you take to sea

            the mute
                    clouds
              file in the wind

            the root wet
              from clean clothes

the trees stand in the wind
  the sea an inversion

            roaring,other places   the branches
            heeled
                    out front of the flagpole

      the attics of houses
    up the hill,   cradles

        emptied   in this light

                breast
                    of a million arms

        snow gone from the ground

      the cars pass off in the wind

        wires   dancing at walls

                                                53
            cool clouds silence the flow

```
              O cloud
              tons of snow   /and power

                  lines

                      a big truck
                          to match this
                      and the inarticulate

                      spread of wind

                          down grade

                      the sudden world
                          in a heap

                              a dog floundering

                          you resort to skis

                              the day will move
```

```
      loneliness, existence
         this is the fine flower   and
        the bodies in a ring
             the geometry

           some substance given the stuff of
              the earth,imitable
                      air
                the graces in a car
                              gun
          and exhaust   the word is familiar now and the curves
             perfect as straight lines

                  Barefoot to match
                          the atmosphere, a
                  plain for the distance,  the
                              slung horizon
```

                    The cats like children
(do   come have supper   The Little League
 push-up)   shouting in unison at
                    boot training   I hadn't looked at the ground
                    for a while
                            no more exhausted
                        than it was   patches
                    of that big snow, since
                    weeks have passed it was
                    an unusual depth, the
                        long lines, and the thought   how
                        nothing would stay much

            It came almost to the windows or
             far enough Others
            to halt the mind   We do not beware of the cold
                from memory, except
            when far gone   The horizon
                        is not there

                            bicycle spills   it
            wasn't a joke He got some pain
            candy in his face   also, it might have been his last,
            he picks up and rides on   That is where
             you stretch and get bigger

            The temperature
            went up and down;
             a few weeks   The tree-stump alive
             in front of me   Children
            come in, men
                eaters Cats
             have outlasted threads, reflections

                    stopped in the night to be
                baled by the sun

            o n   s t r e e t

                and they all
                    wave to me
                when I sit out there
                between their cars

it is music   he
become 5 men
      in a line
                  nor any man

                  to see   time,

         delight of the mind

      in time, the
      harmony

                  at once, going

      a jungle, strange   more
            performance with the lips

      begin
        briefly
      again

   the sun faint or
   bright on the
   tree's bark

      and the air a sea
   where the branches bay

      close part some birds
            stream enough

            and sound through
            boats too

Why do they have two elevators? to
 provide a little mathematical
figuring   the anticipa-
  t'n when it was built
 in the by--gone   one
    breaks down and all the tough eggs
    go back and forth ---   the
        6 floors from the lobby

        empty or otherwise, the terribly various weather
          makes a subject below the roof

        the working faces   the
        hot stuff   I think the air-raid
         is a test   really, do you think
        1,000,000,000 and 1/2 people
        would die   here is an
        insurance crp. on the
        bull.board   and this
        may be the man   window-shade operator
                      the cancer society
          at least has an office,
                    there are no toilets
          in the basement   most
           inconvenient   a chinese
          dentist   his allergy fan
              on the sill   pictures
              for visitors , why a
              lawyer People don't realize

                      coming in
                  from the rain

like a sock in the earth

 holed

wordless room bird

 seeming broken
          from upstairs

the plaster indian   pane

  doorstep the archway

   resurrect anytime Venus

    wooden   remember green

   sun shadow the rain

    spoils a skylight

   in the farther distance up

   a ramp   victory

     waiting
            the shelter
         of old bombs

         past glass   and hat and coat

          trees   corners
                     stand
           harmonic of time

    and the outcroppings
    elsewhere under
      "all that art

    and"the old spring" siphoned
     to the sewage round the park
                sleeve

     enough   cove

    a special exhibition
      for the blind

                        horses

    axe crests

       stones , sticks, native
           against rifles

          against the walls

                    flake diamond of
                              the sea

           the shimmering sand
           dilation   shadow in rain

    black   the somehow disfiguring
           weed   or the smell from
              some deep childhood

        clogged dry strings the
                    periwinkle crust

    of sewage   newspulp   the sea breathing
              out   and in

           to high air

              not visible

         sprays   mountain
            flower in storms

         when under the surface
            the fish bank

                 and give murk

         stems knuckled formicant ice
             water   down

         grass by the sea
            in quiet   smells
             a little way

       dimension of the sky
    vagueness,   where it begins
           the sun rises
         into the 9th floor
                 clean parts of the city

             glass for
         maintenance   smoke
         through the level of birds   flat roofs

         different from window-sills

those crooked houses

the way   standing

the sky packs clouds, mute
like summer ice

stream of trees
wreathing to the ear

a bird in
the porch and over
the next roof

by
the least curve

tangent

as beyond a nest a
window

edge-piece

steepened leaves

the clouds were not
fast   high-flagged visored
hulls   hurrying

a sure place

blue   and now

anything might wait
over the line

and now
a little to the side

it's like the zenith

that purple of

stars   the sun as slow

Asphalt

hello joe
where you go
it's a little neat
in the paving heat

did you ever stand
a multiplicand

    what is the slate
    you anticipate

                     joe cratz

if you never ply   june 24th
i ask you why   1960

    your ducking feet
    should be a treat

The surgical waters,   every 5 days
 a plane goes over

Is anybody dying? I
don't know.   Death or life
   the pipes on a wall, cream moldings

 Differences the whirr
   in being sick

      moments on the window-sill
      the lives of the pigeons

    next door in the day
          hammering
              piles

the steep town
part through hills

 split   day
     season

    with a gun

   the tree shock

    a lane

 and the field a hospital

         efficiently into the air

     the heat
       passes and
             has come again

        the beating down
        of the quieting

            insect

          no more   towers
                    a prostrate eye

                  terrors may
                     be in the sky

                 night's wet
                    level
                      stalks

             pressed row of pain

          a safe high
          part inside

            displaces

                     the shambles

         nice

              shelving of earth

                plates

               the ships
           of the surface

               and flags

          the traffic reach by
           hospitals the
          corridors the patients
            exert   through
             rooms   at
               some elevation

            glimpsing and
          keeping on some easily   the
               trailer-truck driver   the
            retired cop already
          a little heart   the
                              soldiers

            a schoolgirl smiles looking in
          as if searching the window

                  a few days
                then finally stops

      They would not rent or sell the
        building crumbles now
      a fashion in the snow

            fine flakes down all the
               spiralling,past air
                    possible, released
          bird can be easy and cold

            small traces   a single still feather
          keeps flying the long hours
          of whitening walls, the darkness
                         so many wires filled

              something else
                            the thermometer
                small arm to the window

```
     Screaming woman
o god god please god
       beyond wall    angles

   my last night
                  a further
       reminder  expected   now I go home wherever
    it is   Enough plenty
      changing of sheets  these
                        beds high


     The double sashes open
    minutes balmy  outside
    and times the city lay bright
          autumn as
        tenacious buildings      smoke


     wooden  and back up the hill
        old houses   with trees
           heads green bent as some grass


    all  a
       mounting of the sky     the town again
       through the facing window    cars


    lengthen one pane   duplicate
        possibilities  an ice age, say,
     or storms of this level  a twister
         from land or sea might top
              these 4 arms,earth


     and others in life to
    keep the pigeons from
      that side   and a schoolgirl
         who peered in


                     the both of us with a
          surgical wound  i used
          to be sick   felt
             death mounting cool fissure  since
             nice waters  how
          you get through with time
                     the day
          crossed unending
             by night   the two pipes
                down the green wall


        oxygen        suction


           who thought
           the beds


         the interior decorator
           the architects  ?
```

green 30 years

the doctors dress up ,
   the patients in their pajamas
      so much
   to go on
            it's funny when somebody dies
         or you wake up from a fine sleep

      between walls   the light
                  to give
         blankness in shadow

                  this time your water is golden
               I smell like a bad wing

               about to die maybe   I
               who could do nothing about it

   a puddle

   wind in the day and night

      all it takes
                  a single branch
            to shower down
               and a few twigs

               reflections
                  dissolve

            one center
            to rough edges

         walls

               and to see the sky
                  as unreal

               the gnarl
                  in the freshened water

Ply with chocolates
oranges

        Death
     you are attending to

        the juicy imagination
        spreading, silt, but a river

     I woke up forgetting the dream
      whatever I said last night

     the morning again sky
      blue   bend wall, space
                 where the sun comes in

     The clouds move as
                you can see

        how the ships made it
                 by the old clocks

        the outings of wind

          there was mind

          and room for belonging

so many days have passed
                 the sun like a shadow
      afternoon lying out

 there have been lakes of cloud, cars parked in long lines
among houses   a cat

        looks down

     refinements of radio staffed
          coil above a
             fender   a spring   plate halo

        and he hasn't shimmied
                 the tv
                      pole

66

           squint

Washing between the buildings
   Holland   the clear sky
    over the hay-loading
        the clouds'
        brief rise a temperate substance

as if the white mortar of history
   the grounds of people   canals
    mirror the overhung banks dividing
     bridges and is water deep what
      opens the roots as calm

                oblong

    even the streets are shining

  What happened
          to fire, the clouds
  out of hand,   the machines'
     free fall,   sewers
       fouled up, accuracy
         of destructive laws

  Measure of bridges, into the endless boats of water with
   those who would waste

            monument to the underground

  suicide, and the reckless   put it off
       to the next moment

                quiet

        fog
    roof of trolleys
      cobbled
       floods

    night

      mills like a tiller

        varying distance of wind

```
Sound and beat   swell
   funnel of space
 dragged in   earth
 planes eddy, the shaking
  cold,   fish jump the horizon

    slats   factory colors
  we realize    a finish
     there is a tower a
   vast dome
       a dining car   there
          a sliding    seats
         sloped down
         the girders   truckload of stationwagons
  a few  benches at the sea

           or hens crated
                      traffic island

   the oak  starlight glimmering with flowers
      sometimes the sea does turn warmer

        the gulf of cars   engraved

            from everywhere
        the dawning ends of the world
```

```
          sounds like Africa
     badly scarred but beautiful

     legs
       "beautifully scarred "
```

```
         trees
    light   flying one leg

      birds in   the leaves
        which thick sound
             ready ready ready, will

           stream away

            or a taste
           quiet, smelling of height
```

the dead
 light
the walls
  no stream but
 the union
   things are
      the wonder
        tree

   thing see now
              pole corner
         front moon sliced
           sun

    catch light shadow

  a screen flopped
            loose

   it was one of those blizzards, one
 on another

                 the shadow of slow
                         day
                     passes

   the gulls flying around
             ruddering balance

       the wind lit

                    eastward it seems

      maybe it's the stars
        a little lower at night

 a broken-up plane   there is
        touch   sea

               there is
           the wind

   I was disappearing into the sunshine

    you live the

      hopeful
            life

      to see
       depth to the moon

```
     mist of quiet
  up to the clouds blind
  another hot day
  industry,  suits off
  in Yiddish   roll up the sleeves
    after the cemetery
                         the car
       window

  over american toy
    plastic,inc  ink
                 the night developed

    with stars at marine
    supplies    the bridge lifts
                clearing water

  the choppy seas, continuing
     here   they've made it
    the billboards don't peel
     there are years now  gulls
  or lights on their edges    the dining places are fine

       they buy their fish

       70 feet away

       and the brick school
       is quiet with its lawn
        and stone corners, a street at the side
```

great multiple
time   bare
   track
         a line
   of clear windows

      a space set
            the city
         yard
          jaws
             of music   continual waste

            a vast pine
               the town
            room for woods

      how much could you place in the sky

         the river
      what's your shape

            dust floating around   how many
                  thrust down
                     to final seconds

                  as if under the boards
                     mounting papers

         days and nights lower
           beside roots in the earth
               close off the winter, like death

      the splits you go in

         the rounds of idea

         the panels vaulting

         teeth or diamond eyes
      confronted in the street

   Sibelius,   shaking like the rain

            the vibrations wet
            relief
                     there's narrow joining

         or some book   you move on   seas

         the hillsides of the past

            the mouths of burrows   light

            the white shirts there
                         how
             to revolve
             the sea

                    the ceiling, blends
                     in the sky

                    the rim
                            beams

                   buckets of the ocean
    un peu de   deliberate gull
                   above music sleers back,   jog
      t o u r s   horns, pulls
                            away
    d e l a m e r
                        expression
    (my old pal)
                    listeners
                    for the horizon

                    thought
                              gallery
                     or the body

                     sit still, why not
                      arms of sand

             some other time
              you bring on a fisherman

                 it was one end of the beach

       mixed with the forest
                    a dark ground

       a horseman, slowing for the distance
                    to disappear
                    and echo

                  the twig
          thread of sound fold wind

       this union,   00 pieces
             at full scale

        come out a million more names

        above the town

                  at night, where the beach is, cold
                  containers

72

March 8 62   # c f

t year's pink
n   a notice
he wind howled
:erday ,   blew up the tide
beyond the sky-line from trees
hrough branches even more
                    the days before

            out of
    the bark   clear half
    the garage trellis
      two arms of the vine
     tack   crossed way over

        the bare
      sun filling the air
    the roof melting snowcap
      down water   past
      summer, with the rays
        some angle eventually
          slips through
          the flow

          the inferred motion
          from the continuous, your eyes

            followed, or being
                dance

          the remainder was good

          the two windows shook

          and an outer stream on the
          house drainpipe

            covering a side

              those folds
            leak   point of the exit

                    s t r o n g

    the head of his great
    grandmother his
    pillow   dark green
        in the hut   the vision

            here a clock
        breaks out

                        the old
            life, of moments

                    his enemy

        naked sleeper naked
            riser   dream
        of the sky walking out to the sun

                    plain
                dirty green

                    the world
            on its islands

            river a little
                    in the surf

            foam white
        before her eyes, advances

                    trees

                the splintery   hard

                scurrying
                    rain
                    bells
                the pressure of hands

            light from
        your granma

                    beneath skin

            where the dirt got in

        some diet of wood

                through the lamp nightly
            my reflection

                a month   hollowing
                        boat

constant faces
                            out of sight

```
            grubbing

              stand up
                for breeding

              haul

              clear
                the stump

            rubber cushions
              the wheels travel
        all together

            fling stones

              welded decks open
                mute   wind by the bay

                        change
                      the field

                      photograph

              take away the furniture
                woven

            pass of the sun
            how the sun passes

                cooking          fires

                a process from
                    the day

                so it goes

                    maternity

                the animal state of
                    lying down

                    in comfort

                        rubbing a damp cloth
                          closely
                              looking to the gable
```

as time
the miraculous series

so you may awake
to streets in the morning

and maybe rain

the sun already up

June 22 63   # g 5

i sneeze   there

was a butterfly

that was one

coincidence

of a sort

76

one died by this tremendous headache
drowning in laughter
the tv was a gas
some kind of vacation in the wards
        then many went down and voted

              the whole year round
          stars frosty or something
                      wonderful view
              at the edge of your seat

          the moon off
                polluted waters
                        degrees merge
                miles
                  clear sunday

              the one-round fight
          everybody watched
           they had expectations
             chew it , it
             can drop

          tomorrow morning

romance of the moon

              across curtain, strings
                      plaster different from panes
          an even coat of paint

        just outside

          scaffold flutes on the sill

      ?
  you like to come down and watch

                    the gym

    with the sick men

      I know what it's like

    not to get dizzy looking down

              the painter comes through the window
                  to paint
                  the doorknob

            like a suddenly white ceiling
                rest to remain
                        in the eyes

                                        August 29 63   # f g

            days   days   days

                much as you get from
            one octave to another

                                        November 16 63   # c

                we are playing
                a game

♮ for   Jonathan
                Williams

Up and Ahead

an hotel

　a resort

　　　is

　an amusement park

　　an amusement park
　　　　　　of course

　　　a fair

　　　　ground

　　　　for

　　　people

　　　　　with

　　　　　eye

　　　　brows

　　　　and

　　　　　noses

a hole in the clouds moves

the hole in the sky

the earth you may as well
   sit with a foot on the roof
      imagine how rain in the rain
            brief music can be

      piano open as
         eye the sun
   never going off
                  or different times different
                     music of water
            as the snow melts
              carried through the mountain
                the sun has made it white
            your bowstring avoids the steeple, it
            stands clear, as the moon
               at night in crowds
                     your body spread down before
                        clouds
                     a gradual loosening
                  where the greater hill rises
                  hard as your eyes belly
                     cold houses as in heaven

            round around warm lights
                              upside down
                  encroach the sky

         tree disproportionate
          bush flower standing
           in front of your knee you
            ride behind the other
              the broad accessory tapping
               rain on the roof nothing
                inside that could be mistaken
                     the clouds are light
                  holding nothing but mist
                  in the deepening sky I
                  would imagine it's
               the single-roomed house you've lived in

               flowers

                  passing on, white

Futility,
            a voice
          or wind
                high up

    bushes
    branches and then cloud
      leaves

        in memory,the past
            towards its riverbed
          the back of the head, turn
            the neck

            part of the horizon
        the river bends

        the bed its
            deep down

        sun again
          on the rocks ages

          a thing formed by life perhaps
                    intensification of years
            events must take a place a certain size
                print into death

                    tensed life
                    as in memory
                        the gray is the green

            you can look
        straight at the sky

            shadowy bird
            doesn't stop at the tree but goes across
              the road

                wind
                gathered water

            moments grow each direction

        it's a windy day
            with the lions
            among the tossed hills

    the shade leaf
        inside
      like a bird
        over the edge
          a flight   partly through the glass
          on the window it
            fades with the sun
                a cloud coming
                    into view
                slower than the wind
                    where it foots the vine

        I   a m   h e r e

    parked   riding the hill   up my feet

    on the back of the front seat

    a w i n d o w i n d a r k n e s s

        the baby cries in
            the next house   this
        is a neighborhood
            I can't do a thing
                dogs are quiet

    b i r d   m u s i c

we live in the country
    when we shut our eyes

In a corner of my window
    when I lean over the
moon
        going away

with enough breeze
            the sea
  echo of night

        more gulls

            the sun caught
above the tree   robins
            singing
    adjacent parts

the sound

            sea through the horizon
    under the stand of trees

  it comes by on the wind

        flat and round
    earth and sky

                    only the thought
              renews it

                    touching a
              distance   we

                    shall overcome
                    the sunset

                              leaves are borne by branches make
                         all ways   sunlight or moonlight
                         nothing   the motionless

(t o r e c o g n i z e   charge the strip of sun

                                   through the stars
              w o r l d w i d e   from east to west   silent
                                   types of water

              a n i m a l   in places   or time
                                     is not strained

                                   from a faucet   neither
              s t a t e   underground   sound

                                   is towards the horizon

       o f   n a t u r e)   birds
                                         singing
                                    time of day
                                   a bush
                                           but then on the wing

                              they cry

                              eager enough
                              to use our eyes
                                   in love

                              a far blue wall
                              or tangent

                         no billboards
                         in the sky, we may walk
                         the limits of jobs, not too much

                         listening, sing

                         somewhat,   learn
                         what to do with ourselves

motion unperceived   thought
that the visible should be
  this sun   standing water as
stretching the lawn
   day really endless time
would change   broad air
   the branches turning the hulls
                condense the docks
         far away   stir of waves
               makes light   you hear
         cut sound from
            the other afternoons

                     so drowned
                               and
            all sleeping may be a mood

      what damp paper
       wood foggy day
      rain countering glass
            little
                  wind
           brought on down
                   articulate
            equally, the sea
               may sound in leaves

      S u n d a y

                  with clouds
            a few shadows

Time goes where
is light as
I shut my ears

   try and turn   years
      the radio
        comes
              blind

              have
   eyes   the made event
brought further   some
   notable step
              again   again

           turned
off   able to
   fight sound with sound

when the others aren't quiet
   they give you
the means   thought goes
   after speech   high
              lobe   the weather
advancing a turn   too much

words   conversion
      to look at cloud ring
      or blue long day

        side   pockets

      in beyond horizons
              a twig sweeps

      the sky
         as the wind constantly fades
            moonlight comes and
               bathes trees

               the sea sounds

         river open
         tunnelings

               beautiful
            storm clouds,
               the sun
            shines underneath

L i s t e n i n g   t o   s t o n e (s)

If there is silence it's
a long way out
and through

pool the
disturbed
broken flies too
into the air   back

the sea becomes
a truck at dawn

to see the ocean
peace and quiet in the sky
drown view of the city

you imagine the reach of noise
the expanse to hear the sound

the sea echoes   wind
long against man

and through the streets   salestalk
precise, acoustics

glass glass   gas gas
coloring eyes
a system of motion

darkness blowing a wall
cracked in most cases
foam stars
as in the air as
under wheels
of feet

as leaves still growing in
fewer millions

imagination eating
time like a body
mountains on water
wave over and over
vivid on gray
striding streets at
once all that looms
if you find time
you think

if a few things
merge, you may sleep

87

to open your ears
        real music

  on the wire sparrows

  or any other birds
     sit still

     their world dimensional

            more than dogs or cats
            or perhaps men

       and listen

        a moment of stillness

        stick in the ear

         a beginning and origin

       attachment
               of flight

       before the sea's exertion
             to trace the appearing moon

          or stormy as it may be

         an afternoon rain

               how long it can seem to last

     I think it's over there
         the sky through the trees

      I recall passing through them, many

      branches and leaves too
        begin time

         is present

           the moon increases night
           water sparingly

        a new fathom

           a table crickets
              unendingly surface

          the field out back

          different tympanum

                 I imagine it shining

88

s p r i n g   s m e l l

of a spray among
          autumn fires

    the dog
             a leaf up his behind
         stops barking
            and enters the wet

angelic youth
found home

the stepwise leaves
finally rattle

  days follow   days
     raking   slight wing

 morning the sun rises

brick corners the evergreen pool

  you see a mirror through glass

     sky half
              up the staircase
                 the other way

  the trees sound of a river
     birds still hold

              while the river bends
              visible from the plane
                 fuming
                          continues after takeoff

    almost a bird answering the dog

89

        Small, flightless birds
            the voice   far, tinkling bells

        museum

            of sorts,   the rats destroyed

            moving ashore, M i d w a y
    s l o w i s   flat wall of the sea
        t h e
            p o e m   and sky

                        each island
                        rose

                    farther than any whale

                        fins

                    breathing above the waves
                                the mirrors

                heat

                    past sunshine

                    vibrations of air
                        spiders, then birds, settle

                    reflexive
                            man
                        bringing what he can

                    interest

                        in

                    the quickening run-through

                    one thing at a time

                        tides, a large motion

                        small waves give boats

                    menageries
                        from the bottom

                        rock crumbles to earth
                            under rain
                        the seas

                        clouds mulct the moon
                                flats

                        the whale is still hunted
                                in certain parts

90

                            prodigal
                                the deep light

        steam from the rim of a plate
            for easy eyes
            the spent fire

        the sun shines on clouds
            or it keeps raining today

        lakes, rivers and seas

            awareness of fractions

        "Christina's World"

        a skyline, red barns
                are business

        a field of oats

            the head and the body

W i n d y s i d e o f t h e h o u s e

    opposite

        leaves shaking

    some scintillation
        in the grass

    maybe ice
        where a blade might be

            strong

                right near
                    a patch of snow

            a dog appears

            to wander on

                in the fitful air   91

newspaper circling
   the bare trees
 branches quivering
      leaves
            dancing
      the road December

      cold edges

   no gathering
    pattern to
               put behind

  time goes or it seems
    circles of the world
     the crossing of the street

        handfuls

     dust is the eye the
     wind blasting snow
                 brief

      chances of location

           hard

        wintry silence
             of small streams

        change of texture

 the snow drifting

      surface

   increases

        incommensurate

      volume

      Imagine the vast air
           from the horizontal

         the slight winter breeze

            some frame   straight houses

```
       the sunrise
    behind the clock ticking
         as it goes around
```

February 27 65   # i u

```
I feel my life again the strangeness
    it should be the same

  sky grass tree level the eye

    with silence the picture
              bright
       the gift of thought

    it's the old day   speed
           is an idea
       the sun   light so unmoving

         the bodiless roof
       of a birdhouse

          no, it's a
           hose bracket, that's

       right
               being that small
```

June 6 65   # e q ' ' '

```
    you never know
            what is the group
        what picks it up
```

the grown strange

running to childhood
as children to men

backwards to
the next mountain

sorrowful thought
the instantaneous
can't pass the horizon
the stick its shadow the

stone
as history is
a trap nightmare
door
fallen in on
a revelation of blood

the clock
shaken from the wall

lifetimes of wind

the burning insides
of cold light
the close bush
throws out shadow

clouds may seem to come from branches
gnarled
far connection

clear forest
gypsy
hordes
the imagination
the sun comes through

rain the extent of woods

a moment of silence

children striped

smelling the field, freedom
the clouds lower

effortless
continuums
resumed

the movement in the distance

Ravel's fountain
keeps

                    the limits of air

          or the Trout a
          change of wing floors the earth

          General Khanh in his shirtsleeves

            or the ecological position of
                  the woman in
                The Scarlet Letter

                    a tree

              cities are enough
                  riding space
                without wheels

              again and again,the news
                going,hour after hour

                  the clock a vast eye

                                        July 27 65   # j i

          a beast from the sea
             fades inland
           this night
              briefly by the road
            leading on to another
              where waves break
              the surges of leaves
                 through the drought the rustling
                                        dark

                  I seem to see water
                    if things are slow enough
                      they may break up

                        become endless

                                                              95

        to broadcast silence
like the sky

        heat knocks on
          the night

        the sun   blaze
          of frost

        the world through the window

        land slides   the mingling
                of cloud
              gouges hills

            frame

          80° below a plane
                hugging the Rockies

            the bowl
              of roses among other things

                  oars plunged are in
                  bones intent deep

              echo makes it
                      the outdoors

          a dog lapping a puddle

              waves

          are plenty of water

          some birds   reflection broken

              that's a piece of time

                    repeat

                  given tongue
                  a gun

        but if tape the audience sounds
                intermission

        would violate knowledge

              the fuel in the tanks

                  wiring

                  level
                  slosh

horizons of simulation

acts

see   nice lips

words on paper
              trees

ah, the movies
          man oeuvering legs
          at 0g or how
          space different
              continuous zones

          a hand is

branches and
     the nests in them

the open air is
how much distance

               the gutter
               woodwork

          fresh stars

an egg a pond
a tadpole steps from

and warm blood

     the mother returns to
     twigs in the
          light air

     wet or otherwise

          all one as it is

               still
               shape
                    as an eye

              the music,   the rooms

silence silence silence silence sound
            on the walls

      the beach ravelling
       times advance

        or back up
             around earth
           electric poles

       the sun a reflected color
          tropic
            how distance is to some birds

                   in the wind

          fishing

              pinpoint

          the circling air

               food

            the power

              with desperate ease

          food for me hits the water
          without break, the cries

            the meaning of change

        information shifted, player-piano
           on the screen,   the swimming moon

             enters eclipse
          out the window, and other station

          none of us is watching

       the cabinet

                 instrument forgotten

         the clock shakes out

       head bent from the wing

              in a live broadcast

          a case for various things

              dry grassy fields

                    the blank sky

        wampum gulls broke shells

          such eyes
            directed

                        a malnutrition
                          Kenya

                  straightens hair it turns blond

                  scurvy is wiped out

            the dogs come, the group
                      on bikes

              the street comes

              the North Sea

                  studio on a ship

                pivot   spun

                  dark life
                rises
                        leaving the island

                    the dim expanding miles

                    a steady white light
                        they might drive headlong into
                          the mist like a magnet

                  blows   lost bearings

                    nest in fisherman's pocket

                          the wash

" ... distant thunder ... Nearer and nearer came the strange comming-
ling sound of sleigh bells, mixed with the rumbling of an approach-
ing storm ... I gazed in wonder and astonishment ... They passed like
a cloud through the branches of the high trees, through the under-
brush and over the ground ... They fluttered all about me; gently I
caught two in my hands and carefully concealed them under my blanket.
    I now began to realize they were mating ... "

            -- Chief Pokagan, describing an onset of the now
extinct passenger pigeon, in Michigan, May 1850

fall of a leaf
     in June

  this quiet tree rocks

       tangled winds, their places

    calm beach, on the rough

      clouds above the pace

        of any clocks, echo

      some calls, burn

     smell cast

   in the sun
        the bird
      landing
       its shadow it

    came over a roof

     slowing to a branch

      the light shifting

    around here

    out of
   no thing, quiet, the air
    the tree moves

    o moth
    flickering light the
    room like
    no star

the wind
          an ocean
    so the trees make it

      fire

        ages of burning in sight

                  it's a huge globe

            light down in the sand
              to the grass   each leaf

              silence from
                one to others

      what is
        life   now   or who

          may you be   wonder
                this place the rotary
                    good a time

        the blue can the
      lengthy out of sight   the
        large part of
                    time
          the garbage pail
            which smelt

                  gull
              in the clear sky above
              the bird, brown about
              green ground level

                      the house
                    paint gleams
                          out   101

explanation
tangent things

what goes through the head

   what sphere of being

   ideas of bird

    brilliant light

      time,   cleaved water

   flock of birds
            a moment
   of one tree reached

apples fall to the ground

after so much talk, the sea
 relaxes
     its climbed wall

          fill the bank again

      the stars, their rounds
        off the visible

```
5 & 1/2 million
              trees
   annual for the
          T i m e s
       how much is that a
      wood pile
        could not be so
      high   who numbers
         streams   beaten out
          the anvil
              makes good
            work   how many
             leaves or is
             it branches?  comparisons
               are themselves      incidentals
                 in determining what
                    to afford   speak
                        the outsides of the
                    possible?   what
                           goes by  girders have
                      such multiple holes
                        brinks in
                        all-round space and
                     outline    there are things I
                        won't get over   how much
                                    green backs?
                      the curved earth
                        holds white clouds
                      or black, or grey
                         before stars
                       variety
                          in a jungle while
                       in a stand of pine
                           a spruce is rare
                      a dead-letter office
                          is designated somewhere in this
                             complex
                                    well ruled

                          colors for sale to eat in
                           these stores

                              dark glasses

                        shadows of planes in
                                enough space

                         shadow of cloud

                          the sun shines brilliantly
```

        Imagination heavy with
        worn power

          the wind tugging
            leaves

        from the florist's shop

        some silence distanced

some lines I don't understand
to raise the walls like a curtain

the barking dog has the land to itself
the sleepers are all shut in

      pictured california on
        the back of doors   the kitchen
            not lived in

          a plane is aboard the wind
            level

                  mountains space
                    the distance

          interesting folds

          twist
          it

          come
          off   the
          tree

          top the
          poem

almost falling into the picture turned
on   shut
   off   the clock struck

   the table reflected

   dishes, the other side candy, seats

   Which movie?

                  uncertain limits
            of the simultaneous

            I own this box

      a swerve on the highway years
            have become skies

      the elevator, inside
         up and down

                  the car window

            mountain garage

            in a block, this

            cubed shelf on which

            the ultimate building floats

         outside and inside   rooms

            of any purpose   counted

            by any names, the cool

               assumptions, the twists

            of adventure and mystery

            among suave walls, the scenes

               into the night, the lives

            behind the actors put

               the face on

            you're not rushed
                  you've attained the sinister

            what's this all about

                  one spring day
                     the neighbors are whole   **105**

Whitman's cry at starvation
  in a land of plenty

      prison camps   the mean
                South

           six ways
                   of saying it
      the big problem is

         consumption and conservation and population

           population consumption conservation

           conservation population consumption

           population conservation consumption

        or what about
          bringing others in

             conservation consumption population

             consumption population conservation

      I could have watched for a week
        the able horsemen
        with no nonsense

      put the sick with the strong

   eighty thousand to a hundred thousand
   of the wounded and sick
          critical cases
   I generally watched all night

           was with many from the
                border states

             bedded down
          in the openwork of
          branches and stars

      must not and
            should not be
        written perhaps

        marrow of the tragedy
          one vast central hospital
          with fighting on the flanges in
          the flesh--

        how much of importance is
          buried in the grave
            in eternal darkness

                damp
                wind

                    the birds chorusing

                        clouds moving the sky

                                the haze

                            blast the foghorn
                            through the trees

                        car going in shape
                a modern junk-heap exterior
                time   taken up math

                        mach mach I hear
                                a communication

                        the bird sounds watery

                    letting enough things pass

                        thin/thick going up in fog

        a long tongue the kite
            to lick the clouds gods of the sky to
                reveal to,people are thirsty

                        night   day

                        in the Chinese playground

                    how many fires
                        on earth

                        whirling eyes

bright moon   sky

the city darkens
lights up

where are we going

            the cars
            oscillate

        the clouds
            way over
        round bobbing

        visible change was
                    at our speed

        we have the direction

    or the manage of the wind
        surfaces

            the heights   deep
                            outside

    some light   is the fog sea

        clock ticks
    that horn's stuck down
        the street
    there's less traffic

    grow the continuous
    like glass besides
        palings and air

        there are
    the parts of a city   say where
            alleys are shut blind

    clouds really fast

        the distant fades   or
                            is
                        idea

there are random visions in sleep

the washer
  spins   the head off quick
dry
   the near vacuum
 while the wind blows

    on   cloud
      as much as rock

     time so moving

       centuries
             are in the mind

           the ridges scarred

       stone
              builds

          and veins from mountains

         man
           whole does it
                    for himself

             crumbles to earth

          clothes
               fresh   airing

among various hills

      parallels

        verticals

     wires   straight light
                past
      the church, building
         the words,   gathering traffic through

            goods windows

           store banks massing
                   to the side, large

           back of you
           green grown up the air
              crooked the
              end of the street

```
   Like measuring light
speed  while the wind types
nothing, the rain  flung  cloud fast
  huge, the motion, world
                flash of the towers

     the street rolled
             on the hill , past other slopes
       building forms  odd lots

       the bridge once swayed

     by its direction the wind twisting

      the cloud flow  what land
    is a city  surfaces pile   flowers
    or parks in crannies with
    traffic  distance  through the hills

         sun widening the earth
         part of which light a
               quiet chance  total
                       moving

       an hour now
       is clouds they're
               over
                 the whole place
               are level
```

Huge hill, so much
    to lie under
          life burying you

  or overlooks you
field

      the view diminishes
          you come down
        a hole in the wall
         brings quiet the
           water flows
        through pipes there as
         the sun might burn leaves through

          clouds slope
                around the earth
            monsters are quiet
            the tree shapes
            singed spots
          black through the centuries
          twisting towards the light
           they grow familiar cross
             each other

              a skyway   lanes

          channel dug out
             from a river of sap

             or a log
               never floated

             what time
               is   day

         and night changes
          in the weather

          the asphalt road
            calcine a way off

             moon
               out by
           afternoon

               then spreading its light

      in the wind the cold fountain

buildings trees hills
                    valleys
        the fire department shifts
                fog

        clouds shape

        dangling roots
                from a cliff   the stir
            of air is enough
            sound   edge level of water

                    the held on

            growth along the branches

            some faded birds call
                fern reed twigs through the ocean

                    close in 15 minutes

                    a watch small on the man

            one smouldering some while

                        leaves
                            looked after

            tangent horizons and

                the bridge taut

        when you get there measuring gulls and

                the road is paved

                    sections

            the sky become
            endless
            the clouds islands
                    at this level we
                        pass

                    then leaves spread
                    the hills' breasts

Pigeons   the
  heavy rain suddenly
begins
        silences
    between the box-cars
              rails

    levels
        the round clock ticking

    what blood
      lifts it up

September 5 66   # 3 3

    a bird
    bath a cloud
      dropped
      gathered
    mass to a place

        leaning
        tree

      stars   out

Where / when
 the transition made

   the various wind
 with the streets

     hills they ride

       as cloud shaped on
           visible tides

     cars, busses

         earth transmits

     inside one another

       anything's a pile

         there are times gears scream

     and the sun dims the
         clock wall
           minus numbers
             the station goes
             up   still
               into dark

         the regular

   quiet
 as a bird

     the sky fades

       the stars out
           all this time

         air through
         the houses

       a dog is barking
           should there be memory

           the moon wanes too
             to some appearance

114

       copter over at
the zenith
   whirring sun

and how there's been sleep
 in all this wind
eyelids from it, dream

     maybe there goes

           one of these pigeons from the

                ground

                  something

                    the steady sea

             thoughtless
        as daylight

        shifts grass makes
           the earth green
              year bounds on year

the paint smelling
from next door
   fresh tenancy
   an empty flat

 white

        the ceiling lower
      the branches
        massed by leaves you see the
      open
         windows

              now

        men's voices

          double-sashed a while

                part way

           clouds clear in the sun

              or lifted weights

                  birds fly around

happiness   from the year
                    (1820 or so)

end of life   what
  would you like to know
         the nature
       of wants
                  a cloud
        all one   over
        a few big trees
        the whole sky

             whatever put
           time in your mind

         water or light
       at various temperatures it
         rained down

            a substance or
            gradations

          your body stretched

        now there's a long tail
         balanced along the wire

             you take a dinosaur
                pink thing

                  ants
                spread all over the lot
              extensive number

      for the first time in my life
       i see a bird
       sit on a phonepole nail

             trees   weed   clouds
                their due

       gulls

         crickets

       chimneys

          trees

          dirt in the cellar
          smoke clearing the branches

naturally
man
is
gregarious

i see
the houses
pulled
    nailed
together

the air towards the sky
gets thinner and thinner

                    branch turn

  waves on the surface

  the deep pulses

  things
     stirring
   together

        the wind

          fly

      objects

        birds, shove
    out

          thermals

cracked blue wall
        pipe
    water shakes

        rising

    planes muffle
      soar   vault

    surfaces with   time

            blasts of sound
        move some air

        densities   amount   spreads

            the sun courses

        water goes round

    how
    are things

    trees
    without leaves still
    wrapped cool

    a sparrow
    on the dwindling snowbank

    the interval
    of winter

    maybe
    another chirps

```
light  walls  the
     shape of a window

       or more blurred
           the street
           outdoors
         grazed  a long

     hot cold with
        smoke in mouth
             ice

   where the sun shines
        varies

          heavier air

      or light
           minute song

      may imply leaves

        a few clouds
         milling this day

             houses
          are more shadow

             the cut blaze
          turn back such heat

                darkness to ripple
              the line of spring

                  immediate

          the sea's dance
```

```
      bird   skate
      air,    plow
              tree
```

The snow
      bank
  melts
 and by chance it is

 a caved shore

     a river bank

   white gulls come near
     at reduced speed

     flap through the
               trees just past
             the house appear

           so
            they live once
         the egg starts

         cloud, moving and none

        can stay put and
          be warm inside   too long

           time lost
            life   as cloud
           turned down past horizons   rain
             shine allowing

              the sun through
               variously   the light
               and warmth

               always somewhere or as long
          as we must think   but birds

            must add their heat
            to the egg and so
              sit brooding   the sun

            if little enough wet
          is in the sky clears
                      the snow

        it's when the glare has stopped
        and the trees begin more shadow

          to hide some birds for a while

               singing unseen

           though they may do it on wires
                just as soon, where

the air is the same

                    and they move free

                  gulls lining up
                facing the wind from the sea

                  beautiful behinds

                    from flight

              the snow like the sun to stare at

                              March 30-April 23 67   # 8 5

    Head full
of birds   the languages
 of the world
    switching the scenery   the same
  old things

  a crow   momentary
    thicknesses of the air
  are hills   shadows
     below waver
    some clearness   now these trees

       level the lawn
         across the street

       the sun there
            shift the world up out

                whistle in snow

                                                  121

```
What di
 mension  line
   school busses
  come
         various size
    up the street
                 vehicles
     here  the future is

         turning the field

           the uses

                    of grain

            the birds' need

          almost to feed as they fly

            burning while asleep

                 through sun
                     branching
                   cloud
                    shadowy
                      door
                   the children grow

                 wing there   the
                     shape
                 of the whole   trees the
                       present

                        magnetic back of the vane

                  the air stars
                     -a wind-  forwards
                         past

              what directions
                      leaves dis
                            place

          where the sun wanes

              winter

          numbers

              songs

                  concerns

          narrowed eyes time you

             air ripples from sun
```

                    arrows
                      boards
                        the crossroads

                            goods

                      the deeps face
                          the skies

                                              July 11 67   # 1 0 4

        the dying man's car

              the big motor

          He watches the Grand Prix

          He thinks the world is perverted

                                              August 26 67   # 1 1 4

            something to say or
        listen to   the roar

              displacements   it's night

                                            September 4 67   # 1 1 9

              a poem is a
                  characteristic
                  length of time

                                                                    123

dirty work

if you don't give it up

  if you don't play games

      birds flutter

                change to the branches

      or thrust and glide
                  wings closed

                        the sea moves on the wind

                winking
                      air headlights

          sudden legs crouched off

          death a million holes

      a game used to be washing

                contact with light
                  constant water

                    conductors sing at rehearsal

                  lip
                      and hand
                          instrument

                  beautiful breath

                a waste into time

                the bus steams

                a day in the clouds

                    far enough
                  if you go slow

                      this dumpy girl

                  the black freight cars

                        the hungry for

                      games
                      and games

124

                      fragment
                      bomb

the whole earth together

  dirt

  controls

clouds

   holding up air

  water flows

      a surface bent in
      as made

        the moon   rocky

    cast
       at length

      salt washed down

   what to think or
     not to think

    buttons

     flying

    the folks back
  like your own neck as
   cold as past that wall

      to smash the
     head
         on out
  on the tree for you

     years turn stone

     it's geology

       Death
     should be as fast
     as 2 words

        bullets flash
        askant your miles

jewelry cored earth stars

  waters
      over light rock

distance slows bombs

      such places that
      inevitably burst

    in the directions opened where
    you set yourself

     the firmly felt the swing
    the acceptance, dance

      earth matching the sky

      stretched away

      the flamed cave you can't see
      such thicknesses
      till the woods fuse

    till they burn red

     the wonder of moments

        ah what when

      they pass with
      each other

    fade where they are

       fast   slow
       blue   green ... the

       jungle
       with its laws

     past the trees the brush
      the branched turned
         beasts the mined

a girder   a
            building
   earth and sky

 motion   clouds
      you see
          it

          look closer   there   a dark day

             dull fires they

          "roll"their own   take

               the corners

          red bright flame the dead
           picture

                  something
               flashed out

                  a cat's paw

             black as the sea
                 can   be   star

               dust burns
                  up

          what eyes for the spectrum it's
              enough   ours

the strength of a wing

   a bird hits
        the front door

   ah glass

 and the wind flows

    stripped metal

      brightness of sun

          a change spreads in the air

127

how many languages how many languages how many languages my
  mind changed

    the efficacy of words

  member of earth and air
 maple or pine a
   being a cat

      ambled width of the road

    ducks under
        the big car

      shadows   thrusts in the wind

     facing another
          snout to snout

      the sunlight in the fur

    depth riding some puddle

          birds sit
            with trees

        what are
          the hairs

          riffling
            back to the tail

      3 bulbs burn down the hall
        through the front door

      massing goods and swarming people

      The apples we take in

              and

          a few leaves left

strength feels

        babies   how

    unconscious we are   startling

big men on the way

          they run   they

    can't walk far   decline

        the mountain grass   just look at

    stars   knock-outs

              how slow is the distance
                              the graves

        the strong green

            complicated productions

        the loudspeaker from the field

                covers the street

            the phone seemed too simple

          the old man's idea

                he wants to go there

            cutting the grass with gas

                    leaves rising and falling
                        in what winds

        the disappearance of matter

                where is the
                end of a poem

            tired eyes

                the sun travels
                and allows dream

" I was glad that my missile had
been thrown away   "
-- Lord Jim   ch.9

mirrors scattered

you lie down

the sky is clear

or the dark various an

event in your eye

the winds come to your ear

how small each

arrow   what rooms pumped

with sound may be

shut lids

beyond floors

birds sleep in the bush

S. Thomas More said

Tarry while I
put aside my beard it
has not committed treason

canonized 1935

up at the City Gates
the dreamer's face
invisible

garages

  predicaments

 hangars

   tree-huts

something about the Japanese

 all the upholstery on man

     know how to sit

    an empty room
         surrounded by thoughts

     the walls hold shadow from night

             openings

    jet

      prop

        the sky

      the sunlight cross roofs, fields, a

        familiar thing

from the chinese laundry
  mat lot
 on the east coast
    brown leaves
   Hallowe'en

      wan dead tooth   there's
        indifference

    the old people themselves

the street

plastered with leaves

let's

actually twist

the shapes made real

Silence!
except for the
cold storage motor
the oil burner
the clock

and the big plane
briefly, somewhere

any size   its end

now there's
a morning

sparrows eat seeds
the energy
to push air

how many is one I
scour the
countryside

nebulous

front of me
a happy wave

the plow

polarized

cool here

that's all figures
  the car volume more sun

        a gull coasting

    the porch

    going along alone

      straight roads

      poles march

    name gradations
  the skies far no angle
        above the signs
    or how many   that make
        the maximum

      what lights are there
        before stars

      to think all the time

          spokes

        these fumes
                    it's
      mirrors that tilt
                    things

    the curb round fender

    hard now immobile lids

        inside down and outside up
      morning whole cat poring the cup

              the gray sea what seasons

those shades are from trees

a bird from the clothesreel
a yellow / leaf

thing is ours
back yard

changes of view
nothing we say   flat

the wind
the railroad tracks
harsh silhouette
the moon's eye train

half complete steps in
vanishing cloud

There is no community

he goes to

Work   mornings

the motor fades sway the

numberless   towns

the ol man steps
at 2 a.m.
wind cloaks the house

it's no matter

blown hard   what times   the

snow flying
down headlong
rests

not much

milk of earth a well
   water   stars

a wind   to breathe

hidden years by the window
        smell of rain

       the light wavers
                        and air
              winding to silence ears

       far vibrations the mouth
          reception   the plane shakes

             Iceland wood

             Canada stone

       a fine brown sparrow

       or some few leaves hung

                        paired dust

           dream-like
  varieties   the real

   morning moves on the earth

  the rising moon, the sea
   such distance holds apart

    Who is it

         the man that fails

         the man that failed

       he gets up
                there used to be fields
            and walks through here

       remembers the opening days

       and weeds were a wall

             among the houses

exhaust burn piles the road
like clouds   then a high truck leaves none

then a school-girl

        the sun was the morning

    a fog-horn sounds

                    there's the overcast

        they still use
                    things

    wonderful !   wonderful!
        the separations, powers in
            the whole

        there can be

                        the sea
                            tumbles
                        down

        three green strokes

        the light of Holland, of
                    the States
            the pavements

    by the water

        any
            place

                cloud in it

        slow
        river into
        the moon

        you forget the heavy
        industrious

            memory, some
        good in itself

the big black car
   absorbers pull up
    the rain
          myriad streets

  or these sounds
    where the smells freshen
  from the earth

     the piers hold

       and splinter

        some boards apart joined

     ah, drizzling

          the drive together

        intersection
             point

       other corners withdrawn

     zig-zags

           cannon centuries past
           had monstrous mouths

       night facing the sea

       corbelled wood

 A fence by the road-side
          a tree

     there is
       some ploughed land

      across from
        dark woods

     he rides through the low stream

      such brown water
        the rocks abut

        the blue sky whitens   137

The world that was, the glass

King King King King

of fashion burst in your eyes

sanitation
men

all the green
over the arm

what's experience, these
... passing time

trudging the newspaper
looks ahead

opens to jaws

academic my
dear

the visibility   something

that can happen
does and

the poor wife
couldn't eat supper

how to assemble anything with

flowers in the hair

some kind of accident

Nobel

big shot
on the bus

these
years

back   with
the simple song the heart

smoke the
air

outdoors
clouds turn

ever shoot somebody?
--doll in
a mini-skirt

                    I ran her over

                              arms

             smashed light

                what you think of the garbagemen

                                   nesting
                              under the blue eave

                     Nothing act-
                                  u-
                                 al-
                                  ly

                  some great fog noise in the head

                              I could perform

                                        May 14 68   # 1 9 8

             a toy cart
                up-ended, a

             begging dog

                quiet

             birds echoing in
                the heat of the day

                                        May 17 68   # 2 0 1

                  t r e e s

             birds flying like waves

             up and down

             in the wind walk

                the porch rail

                                                            139

marines
       futilely
   by the skin of their teeth

        types

      blood
        slide

          near
            here's

        the photo
                       images
                   form

          time

      you enter it

      far away

    white clouds in the sky

   far from these birds and green

    the most sunshine

empty but still
   trashbarrels
 back of the porch

    lattice

  the cool dirt

          shadow cast under

      clamp puffing quartered cigar
               as he mows
               the grass

          to be odd business

          power that's noise

moon

arithmetic
in the night

rain

birds   birds
what little nudes ripping around
    feet, feet , feet, feet
  really headed somewhere

house

heard carpentry so

unexpected
        firecracker made you dribble

    july   you
            get shot

how soon the beach on the way there

  a mother calling some kid

    by fetishism we
       lose"control"
    (of all the land from to)
          wild death, blind
          as most lives

                make the idol
                disintegrate
                        ourselves

    within doors
      some hammer and nails

never known how to keep
      even the trees
          in mind

    how long the airports last
    how long the monasteries

  deliberate stillness

    in winded birds

141

                                                  July 4 68   # 2 2 0

      beautiful books

          again and again it's

              the complicated world

                                                  July 10 68   # 2 2 3

          glimpse
            of the wailing wall
                      on the tv
                as I went by
                  through the living room
                      with a jar of glue

                                                  August 5 68   # 2 3 3

      clear-cut shadows

        a bicycle by its motion
          erect in the street

                  appeared and disappeared

                  trees stir in the wind

                                                  August 15 68   # 2 3 7

      A bird from somewhere The wind rouses the tree
            there is only green in the sunlight

                up and
                  down
                nothing
                    sound ends
142

the roofer's truck   lumber projecting

   the seat   the shoulder   the road

ladders   red flags

     hands busy   more than two

   any old radio

        tunnel music   concerted
                  voice
                          fine, uh?

        end of a job, ropes

             the dashboard there
                       inside

        "take a last look around
            to see how it squares

I spend half an hour ringing the bell

           there is no door

        tongue   nothing at all
   moving
                       a plane twisted

           the boy downstairs
        voice going up the scale

        and a rooster crowed
        too early or too late

so many cars
  keep the road straight

    tossing branches for
        the eyes   some

        leaves adrift

    what wind there is

    the cars' incessant
        noise

    like the ocean

    distances

        bodily

    dimensions

        smell it

      holds together

        certain degrees of

          the next town the next

              junction
                    it bodes

          tomorrow's wonder
              more or less pain

          the all-night traffic
        wakes you up
          too much or
          often enough

            and you keep going
                with things   the

              more   it's a
              discovery
                  of change

          like what was behind that

        brick wall
            or fence
          not
        just an old back yard

            like dirt
            and bottles but

there were birds

detached   passing

and you heard the sea

was there nothing to that?

the lights
   almost continuous make

the window a
   peculiar corridor

neither long nor short

in no direction

September 13f 68   # 2 4 6

What is
the muscle-bound
   in me hides the
consum(mat)or of time

      Where
   do I send pain   Who

   can travel light

   the inner sides of the tracks

October 11 68   # 2 4 9

ALL THE EXCITEMENTS

   a brand new car
    is a brand new car
   I'll see it in the morning

the whole round of earth

overlooking

your own back yard

                abstract
            a geometrical rock
                    in the various

                    the sea dripping

                        mobile at
                          the sides
                                faces
                        to the towering skies

                        fish and land
                        creatures ships
                                symmetry

                        the sun up and
                down   light spread

                    stars   rain or a moon
                        band   the silent clouds

                a shape to cleave the waves

                                any
                    size you can imagine

                    and made parts

                    inside are crowds

                    flatter and flatter

                    holed distance

                    arms of a tree

‡ Philip Whalen's
VOYAGES
a TransPacific
    Journal   ‡

146

Pain you
  shouldn't think of, even

 when you have what
  shouldn't be there   my

      numb thumb

       such a big bandage a

        careless cut

     foreign material

              chores

         lying lightly

           to be got through or
           enjoyed?

      an awful lot

          don't puzzle

           how you can sleep and
             can be the more

      roaming the house
         something loud   where
           the wind is   outside

        the miles down to the beach
          any length of time

        imagine the extent

the strange   the familiar
 headlights   eyes

   we loved riding
   the back of the truck

    the sleigh on its course
   coming down the hill
   spilling so many ways

        we could never jump

      a flying start

          it was
             always
         suppertime

          the bells at
             sunset
                there

        the horses

      every night the power
                sleeps wakes up
             in the morning

the mass of leaves is elusive
             ungraspable   Zukofsky's
   but they have their substance   <u>A</u>
      even as single things

   rain the wind carries
    long as it falls

        you want to see a man
             but what can he say?
          it's all in the head

      a flock that in time has
                come together

Settling out setting out   for
          roadways   jackson
     you are where you are   mac low

  at the end of a process
      what you've done

   all those positions aims junction

             houses

     a firefly in a field

      night grass approaching dance

    too numerous, old

       bent the precipitous

            look down one
         gathers dreadful
               trade   freight

         ships   Buddha
           on the wall or edge of
               pandemonium

         spreads peace with
          certain fingers

           since he sees such fingers with
               upholding them
             level and open gaze

         and we can watch
           a circuit is made there
         almost closed when
            we have to be, the
               flowers
                       seasons
                  that
                    we are

```
     the night goes    the fog-horn
   in cold weather        steam

     and the mines    how black
       accidents are      all
                                places

       slow up, round, lengthen

   a shade    still reception
             of the idea there

           making a snowman

           how much dirt

       mute    time passes

           the stars set in front of the house
             and rise at its back
```

February 16 69   # 2 8 8

```
                      one little

                      thin saturn

                      spiritual rin

for daphne b                g in the big life circus sin
   marlatt

                         dig   down

                         some other planets
                         beyond the pale
```

February 23 69   # 2 9 1

```
                 oil at st.a barbara

           grass-roots
           sky-high

               violence
```

```
           earth mined
```

the pastorale

  symphony

the snow is
         white   white

      in the yard

       sunshine

        the wind   sheep

   what do the clouds graze

    in safety as

     a child feels

      heedless

       of indoors

   positioned   slow   like the aerial

   half blown down

    by the freak blizzard

   what this place may be

    unreally cold and wet

     when the music was conceived

     in the air the slant snow
      the bird rising away
     from the wild and bare tree

I forget the color
    upstairs, the aerial
on the roof

            the trees

    half-way to the horizon

        the seas
            falling beyond

    3 p.m.

    flag waving

        signs

    fire-escape
        shadows

        dust flown   brick   the tall

    basket
    bull's-eye
    bounce

boy and girl
joined up again past
the smoking trashcan

    waists   each other

controlled fires

    2 long containers
        jammed in

            none too fast NOW

        the man who's come out
        the back of the one-room store
            in the parking-lot

                lower jets and   and
                    trails blacker

y o u   k n o w   w h e r e   y o u ' r e   g o i n g ?

Life the placid
        time-bomb

            how long the
        other end of the fuse

                earth
            coiled up in

        how backward running

        brake to re-enter

                you eat yourself out
for the   all ways by the tail
    Webbs

                    it's all moving   the road
                    taking you away

                the desert side

                            gardens
        and all

                    the flood

                earth temperature rises
                        towards
                    the boiling point of water

                    with power plants

                    cool lighting and fires

                    or fluorescents could dim

            Canadian to Australian a
            comparative distance
                            the earth bends

                travel's a descent or
                        pulls   or a tendency
                            among the stars

                    it gets heavy
                        it grows light

                feathers are good for clouds

                    and rain streaks

            the artificial cavern under Denver

                the poisoned lake
                        the shivering land   153

sea smells
   smoke
   weed

 the sufficiencies
 of the past

flames shot up through the roof just afterwards and immediately
  spectators grasping the magnitude
      the situation

      total
      edges

    clapboard
      points towers
     shingles
        in and out

     sky sound the back
      ground stars where
       actual land

    bushes unsinged

   thousands
     of minutes later

   700-foot front
     to a building

    sand spots of the golf-course
     any place burned-out tv loot flanks mounds

       taking heat off to fly

     hour-glass partial moon
     incised to climb

    intricate curbs road section
     a bike tar
      black limousine

  hoses couldn't reach low flat
   across the soft sand

   glittering night

    visible miles
     days

   brands four feet long

   so many windows

towards grass and hedges there's

one spray vs another the
                        finite

the nearest water main unbroken
      a few hours before

good as ever the
            local said

a surprise

   train whistles
   often enough

      memory

         in the eaves birds, the tries
               to rescue eggs

      the seen the
            sky the
      to be seen

   colors

      breezes

July 17 69   # 3 3 5

      ominous

      sinister

         the rain

      smiles

such screechings of brakes
what was it a
mile away maybe
thick of the night
from home

how long was it with us ? ?

beauty shop

groceries

blanks

sales lots
get your ticks
do-nuts
dentist offices

edge tools

table supplies

work

work

work

the lower the more open
to the skies

the wind blows

across the corner lot
the grass in the graveyard

husbands and wives

```
my back
        to the front of the house
          inside inside
        what is this sense   of moving
              through life
```

```
snow makes   a slow   season

however varying , cold

      shifting,     remaining

          clocks move

                    different circles

        gulls huge among the airy

          roofs hemmed out

          maneuvering
                      weight seems to

          loom and stalk

              they

          won't be far

            wherever

              winter goes
```

```
          co-op

            wind

            ows a

            door
```

                    the apple gone

                no more tree

                    its shape
                                its shadow

                    streaked skies

                    the birds on the ground
                            picking up crumbs

                    sun   rain
                        bellying cloud

one woodpecker it seems

                                    the last time to the right

                                        flashing doors

where they took down the green-house

  sticks

            tarred paper

        odd nails

                        flowers grew

            quite a few fires

an old phonepole lowered cut
                                    some use

                saw-horse method

                        electric hand

            bolts

                            power

            a neighbor's pear
            in days frozen the wild

                                bend-ups

                            over

            sheered off

            joint by joint
                the bridge far in the air

                    distance beyond sight

                    stump   stump   stump
                        level

        Can't hold
        both hands

          fine print

        never mind

                                        March 10-1 70   # 3 8 2

birds the
  warmest blood in the world

    keeps hopping

      powerful breath a ground

          target while brooding

                      the
                    positions

            man's
        growth precarious birth
            to soar in the mind

          so big to the earth

                    whole   parting

            active   wake

      all the dimensions

          a great head   of

                                        March 14 70   # 3 8 5

          the radiator
          simmers
          down

          after a few years

          it's quiet

          it's almost dawn

                                                159

        how cool may the night be

intersections of forms
                areal
      the world's parts move
            a magical shape

        in   out   of

          all

          so cloudy
            is change

          fog is gone
            leaving the ground

            rain drops

              the sun penetrates

              certain things

                though some slide off

churchbells

    years ago

      minutes

      while storms of men, say,

        last night, some

        freshness of tack,

        not to believe,

        nothing but war

          is war, ex-

              haustive death, a wind

              rain, starlight's gone

                blue, nothing alone, birds sing

imagine you see rain

dark place

and wind

on a bright day

crossed self   hand and foot   re strained

abstraction
   in the dark

            d
           e i
            a s
              s
               e

or how much to
        live

      how many
    times
            breathe

to decide death
   besides life at

   what time

               slips by

      the sun and moon, all
         their distances

   may fill our minds   yet

      what corners
   can you run free in

      how much do we
         have to know

               for the habit of hours

All matter

standing

build up

wave to wave

good and bad

time goes

leaves changing shadows

the wind fails   what paths

I fight nothing
there are no weapons

separate clouds

traveling   in the years

the sun, depths,
varying, mass

the window opening

no,   already opened

nothing but the wind up

My god   the
      proverbial

we drive in

      and
all are mowing the lawn

         trimming

         snip snip

      the firetruck

      this distance

      scream

      my   town a giant

         place

            embank

      the day of the party

      trees in the wind

The imagined, returning
      what is
            endless song

spraying up
    the tree
        down
      wind sounds
    the straight no
    mix
            clear water to the eyes

     it may be a wet
    bird
            elsewhere   time later   how

      to work

        singing

            through

        tough branches

            space

        they keep in the years everywhere

    various quiet like the sky
      a steady plane moves

I saw a squirrel

    I might be
        those two kids

        I saw
        a cat

            both
        on the ground

        there were different

            sky and trees

                flights sounds

I ride I
    don't believe in planes
           what purpose there is

      various principles

    tremendous craft

          until my end
                    the surface gets easy

                           infinite air circuits
                            merging

              clouds like our wing

                out the lined window

                  maximum length every

                    light spreads

          typing

               clicks

         no open window
        in sight

          a while

        the weather
           hot   brilliant

              fire-escape

          as we say, the air
            filled with light

              blinds down

rain

curtain

birds and

thunder

You ride for some hours
                    stalagmites
          clouds   cities

Yes,   it's

    liquor

      I smelled

          that breath

            nothing

            lost

cars arrowing
increasing traffic
  each way
  by
    the funeral
      home
    daytime
    hour by hour

a temporary language

   as temporary things

    and poetry the

      math.. of

       everyday

        life

           what time

    Of the day is it

      lad what

       have you

        to do with

         or gotten

       done

       ‡ for

       D Gitin

spread-out constellations
      dark
    areas
       all
     together

        far and near

          points

‡ after
Shiki

Coming to see the cherries
        he had his money-bags stolen

it's too bad

the man from the country

‡ after
Bashō

the moon shining

deep

air

waters

dreams

stirred-up

leaf shadows

Quiet grass
                    ‡ after Bashō
still air

rocks

the locust

cries

      ⧧ after
           Bashō

u n k n o w n

    tree

    flower

    scent

"I cannot see what flowers are at my feet
Nor what soft incense hangs upon the boughs,
But
               "

      --said John Keats

Don't cut
 time to pieces
Let it stand

   inside invisible

     again and again

   it will work as it happens

      your eyes open

to negotiate the ocean drop by drop
  if there were time

 it goes on after us

 the sea extends

                    a dark day

                 all this time

               clouds

                    birds in

                      the air

                          and it rains

                     trees

                  a few leaves

                       with

                        stand

               R u i n

                    M o u n t

                 k e e n   V i k i n g

                 M u s e u m

               M a n   h o w   C r e a t u r e s

             B r e a s t   t h e   e a r t h

     What stuff

          cloud wrack

          real time

          miracle

          bean stalk

       whoever lives in

his father's house

the phonepole line the floorlamp ticks

   clair de lune
       as the clock

    various   curved coastwise
     order   stretch
           in mind

        as how little water
      memory, can make a flat
       glint it passes
          out and in   shade

       a hitch

              gets brighter and brighter

          load in transmission

           musical steps

       the whole time

           different
           miles

            as repeat   selves

       or nothing to imagine far
        beyond the nodes
                struck
                   brightness, measure, soft

         niagara keeping
                the flow
           of its fallen mass

REMBRANDT LIFE TAKES

to see
dark   the
 invisible

   time's
long enough you
    remember

   you thought it was
   as it is

Music is human in the event

        the sea curves

            (drag light
                    in the earth

    the great sea is orchestrated with men

        the wind and the waves

        oil slicks

    trees stand

        dead or alive

          branches in

     all its gradations

            winter pass off

        again big

        round on the roof

         long feet gulls

          when they fly they cry

             thought flap

(resting or doing something
Southern California, Feb.9 71)

highway

low in the wind

breaks   open

as buildings   in

pieces   or varying masses,

binds, to keep each other on the move

oil and water

empty spaces

and many things piled up

the

underground

seeing or

belief

smell

you hear something

what's a dense field

what tides

and the air takes the sun

deep as it is

```
common sense
   experience              ‡ varieties over
                             enigma
the milky way
  river of heaven                - for L N ‡

            elements
    out there
    a pulsar
    intrinsically winks

         all the route
         not imagined

         the naked eye

      could not discover

                         time

         so much

                   or any thing




                                        c. 1971


         rain

         morning
         jungle

but the night
      music

    I can't snap off

         a loudness between

         it's almost the feet


         with all that kind you may like

         I will
               bring back

         waiting for the sun
                    degree
```

```
motor
   some process
simulates the sea
                  's
      sound

   a result

   cross
   winds

   salt
      is harsh

indoors the refrigerator
                   once in a while
      hums   a wall

         and voice
                   mechanism

      the earth is
        how
      lost in space
```

```
   nuggets

   kernels

   landing

   birds

   farther

      the sea shines

            space
                  seasons

      trees move
         air I

      starlight

            reading   can

      with enough glass
```

snow

    flakes
      are single

down

  to earth

  but they light

    on others

    or a tree

     living still the

      current of air

     the sun diffuses

      some steepness

       however close

     twigs

        it first snowed

        a while back

    two, four mirrors

    windows

    trees

   a wave beats

   a wave passes

   up and down

idea of

some
        thing certain

the dark sides of clouds

    the sky a sight

            movement

        things   fly

    nearly still

    in   and out,
                on trees
    some wind   question

        what's all ways

    or a rock, struck

            lines in small detail

            similars   large

        there's always some wind

        rainy

        days

        hours

        nights

        whenever

            the trees stop

jaggied
   potential

abundance
associations

 farm
  country

 seen from a plane

 lightning

   we turn away

 fuel dumped behind us

     related speeds

               we don't know

         headlong   palpable

         over what rooftops

         roughnesses

      across   lots and streets

pi r^2 many
 lead cutting
  corners no
 place tweet

     tweet   tweet

                    cable-car
          many
      for the ride I
          guised backwards   my
                          age

              us
            here
              multiple
                hard
              rails up at
                hand
                  motion relative
                geometry direction
    ‡ f o r   just one alternate
                      seats taken steep
      b . ‡   hill sides
                      line of sight

                  how old
              is this one

                      a way

                          where

                  what is
                  home

            in and out of a store

                  swung norms

                    lunchings

                    different
          glances wholes trip
        as some clocks working
          endless reflections
            left someone
          the half-length of a street
                    turned
              climbs on
          spreads up forward look
                what map

              with the wind

                  square

                      shouldered

                          corners
                                              179
              some watch on the level sky

the music of

  the sea

beyond

the wood

    the wind blows

      the leaves

        they stay

      there such times

     roots spread

      flower

      face the sky

        sphere

        ah the seed

         not to choose

harsh half-ton

  ash barrels

    dumped

     in the night

      and the rain

     thunders

      shake the world loose

       here and there

       the sea rides

       up and down

       under

paper

  a cut map

    beautiful

   land

    beds

      tree

     the air

       to dance in

        time

      what ground

      stretches out

       dancing,you feel like
       dancing

        so many winds blowing

     forest   the mind

      flight

      the sun

         on the open

        then the earth

          wall

Of a new aper man

ever ear

with a straight face

denouncing Shakespeare

as an Anti-Semite

by an ospital window

lying unknown

in 1960

an oceanless

patch of sun

wherever did
it go

mirrors

methods of flight

the world

smiling

big Pacific

clouds cross faces

        so muggy

    in the thread

        sound

            night

            siren

            and way back

                    away

                    when

O what

        orientation

        questions

the reality behind
 the sky the
    branches

        wind   roots   seed   the tree

        spread

        merge

    A s l e e p

        mummied

    what space there

                                        183

    was is

an original

                eye

a reverent
                                    c e z a n n e a
            eye
                                        c a t h o l i c
        wild

        discipline
                                            u p

                eye   o l d

                eye   h i l l s

        what you

            see you

        settle

            on

                moves

            do something

            feel

                a

            victory

        or mountain
                        what

            you can't

                go through

                nor replace

                a road

                    a like

                        curve

pigment, air

  biblical in the

17th century

    the fishmongers   boatman

  each fief

  A i r
                        F o r
in the yard of
                          S a m
another house
                        B o r a s h
    a phone bell

  miles away

      in
        doors

    a small willow
      by the front steps

    Aggre-
      gates

     pow!

     sail

      dark

       air

        the night

        Arrangements

        pistons
           products

         the straight
             ways wide

          space

broken cement

all through the town

lumps

earth smell

out of the wind

no, flowers

pots

next in the cellar

rubbish

all over it

took a bit

to fix it in space

corner

fences

lines

cars

bicycles

metals

the stair

well

round

in consciousness are

    forces

  how anyone sees

    things

    hours sun and planets shape

      each globe

        air

        moisture

         packed rock

          the sea's pound

          flowering trees

        how you might think

        across space

August 16 71   # 5 1 0 a

    grass path

     mountain

    a pond

    rough edges

September 12 71   # 5 5 7

   brigade of the rain

    all one way

      subside

how it works

 forces

   find out

  the wheel

what's what

    bucking

  like magic

    rings

      the known and the unknown

   is real

      the foghorn
              blows

   the wind or the sea

     stirs

     morning
             is beyond color

 Funny it

   leaves you

  look at yr

    the baby
       you say dis-
          covers self
              like nice
                soles

       the friend
          is no longer

shadowy

   gesticulations

  on the lawn

      young tree
        trunks
     a little in the sun

       leaf
           shapes
      across them too

beautiful

   the light is

 all one way

   after

       noon

   where it falls

    most of the earth

    unknown

    to us

   clouds are idle

    spaces

a car door
is smaller than
a house door

bang

the
        morning

earth smells

            drive

                off

        birds sing

        calendars
            older than clocks

                    mystery   through
                    top and bottom

                memory be
                    eyelid
                        move

grief   dry the

            council

        far away

        inveterate   interest

            some dust

                the stars are a million pieces

                    some million a million

                people suffer the end

Beyond pages
      to have things whole
    There are millions
        on earth

                less fish in the sea

                it still roars

                To be is involved

                    such words that hold

                    times in the mind

                        I saw a bird its
                        food in its mouth

                    when does it rest

                    when does it fly

            birds

              tree standing

              hair

                snowstorm

            whiter

                whiter

                white

                white

                  thickness

                how far

                                              for
the kids in the back seat   houses   Paul

    past   throng

      on the sidewalks   that

            headline is obsolete

        papers

            under wheels

        bridge flatbed

          ramshackle

              years ago

            clotheslines

          in roof islands

          hammer and nails

                man must eat and

            cannot go naked

              in this climate

        as slow

          near

        as time

          here's snow

              fall while the sun

                goes back and forth

a new
 ballgame

        paper is fresh
                under arms

        the street to
             be sudden

                front

           right, it's

         smooth driving

           smooth walking

              parked

           a crowd

                the sea

              always retreats

                        there
                         ahead

              always

                     comes on

              resonances

          a few garages

                earshot

            different

               times

               birds

                   the wind

                   sound

                  from leaves

             the moon

                is

            miles from the air

                                                        193

            trans
                  formed?

The great impact of steam

  motion

gusher

dam

  where you sat

    volt

  progress

     something to stand up

    the road dzzz

      rocker

   milling

       the wind

   cloth

    figure

   manifold

    put out

     wheels

       contact with
          lightning

    such principles of equality and
     fraternity as had seldom been realized
      hitherto   except
    in small cities and tribes

     revived and applied

    trying to see

    what do you see

reflect

world corners

mountains ride

and wind among branches

leaves
different lengths

a wave bends

moments

what purpose

sights

sounds

visions

the earth goes round

A full life

taken little by little

not all at once

you gain time

the pieces wholes

history

romance

by the leaping

fires

195

of

W i n t e r

3 black figures

in the street

  all
      turn out

    to be
      schoolgirls

January 4 72   # 6 2 2

Looked like she was roller-skating
    while it rained
    the sidewalk
    full of reflections
      I imagined it close

January 22 72   # 6 3 1

Many lives

    budding ahead of

                us

  the tree
      branches enough

  the leaves

    fall out

      on the wind

January 29 72   # 6 3 5

It looks nice in the snow

    getting lost
    where I used to get lost

February 22 72   # 6 4 6

  the moon

    in

    the
     sky
      after visiting

    the wire

     the wind flows

March 8 72   # 6 5 1

thick snow

  in the air

merges   time

    on the ground

    it keeps on

      the earth holds

March 16 72   # 6 5 2

    driftwood

  the sands

    a tree spreads

    dirt is

     hard grains

197

Hide and seek
                    indian
cops robbers the
    walls waning
                        steady

            paint

    verticals

        hard to see

            corners

        the wind

            leaves

        the sun

            ladders

        pot ragged

            what days

        scaffolding

            hung   too much

            to watch

            all sides

                of men brushes

                    weigh locks

                flat plane

            then cloud

        damp air

            and there's sandwi

                    chilly

        at the beach

            seasons

                perceptible clock

        the lee

            shifts

                    the windows

                       the weather

                    pole flag vane

                          across the street

                    the shadow sucked through rapidly

                       at noon

                    the trees are so high

                       the sun tangled

                          but we have a firetruck

                             really resistant stone

                                        March 24 72   # 6 5 5

Take it

   every atom of me

   belongs to you

      across distances

      one space

         a photograph of a dam

         or a morgue

         or hospital

         or anything

            on its side

years are

  wood
    staircases

  the same

      public buildings

      have some guts

        in the wind

        so many ships

        again on

          the horizon

        radical designs

            you see them change

  s h a p e

    s h a d o w

      e l e m e n t s

            m o v e

          p a p e r

            t a r

anything
        has to be easy enough
                to get done

single

notes

sung

zigzags outline
           the

n dimensions

the world

far corners

itself

life

room
for flowers

shaft
the air

winds
move

dimensions

distances

directions

p l a c e   t o   p l a c e

well

    life is

        moving

        like the wind

            now

                blowy

            vacuum and weight

        anything

        at all   there

        see mountain

        shoulders, confusion

            crowds of men

            borne away

        when you slow down there's sound
            the ropes buffeted

        against the flagstaffs

        rest area

            many placards

            and walls hold

            gravelly like rain

            it may be dust

                at

            the base of the car

vacation

cabins

in the morning

all over
you realize
the trees above tall

swaying

steep up the hill lines
there's a good view

a road sign later
fast you can stop
and eat

it's motionless enough

and the sunshine

a bicyclist along the way

changing

June 23 72   # 6 9 8

advancing

rain

with the wind

in the leaves

the mica   clean on
the walk

                various complications

    everywhere the light is
        part of the sun

            by day

            the stars are invisible

        from stillness
                the air waked

            gold   coal   water   gas   which turns

                earth stripped

                            we change
                                each other

            in the trees

                the strength of cross

                    winds

                    and then sunlight

            in the shadow

                cross

                    winds

                    sunlight

The days the motors burn past
    the houses ,   under the trees

        repair smoke   your

    shingles

            all grade 5 on
        the beach trip   in a bunch

            teachers

        whistle

        steady

                heat

        slow

            map

        calendars

        if you see it
                might be
                        easy

        how
            anyone works

        in the haze

    Now

        the eclipse

            traffic

        bicycle

            the night rise

                in

                one space

perfect
strangers, dining
     in the air   together

          tossed   out
            the window   the world

          Gluttony deeper
                    Lust

          as plate keeps
            precarious
                trays in

                    and there are
                delicates still
                areas such
                    foot travel

                aisles lead
            ramp taxi
                foundations off

            cats turning
                al-
                leys to sleep

                in
                    light   the

                        earth seems

                    to run

                    gotta go

                    ta la

                        most things

                        roam legs

                    novel experience

                    get stuck

                vertical direction

            make and break

                distances

                    smelly roofs

                    ride over

                     to the walls raised the
                         works

                           face people, their panes, the poor

         food brought through the mouth

                                   dichotomy

               young

                     old

              around

               where

                  gunmen

                            deflect

             bound to drown

                  enough

               stakes other

                     fantastic

                       sums

                          out of mind

                       tend to your business

                              July 20 72   # 7 0 6

          How you
            stand

         for your
                   self

            one quarter
              the muscles
                the face

               mouth

               changes   **207**

wheels

  familiar

    turned

     light

      front

       roots

        streets

      a kitten

        stretching

      in the grass

         sun off dirt

          you can't see stars

           wires

            kept running

          in places distance

           gives out

            moving

             the sea

              so many circles

              you leave traces

               birds that pass

              imagine the wind

              through green leaves

             the sky brought near

               open full

                silent branches crossed

along walls

reached you

figure things

the solid

the group

life

span

the world where

energy goes out

binds

displaced

settling

near and far

develop touch

the wide awake

how much a squirrel is
in the road knocked dead
the same generations they
going around the wires

up the pole
down the tree

not leaves
call
the
patrol wagon

after how little blood
from far away slow

an action of your mind
is to take your time

when does the sun come out
or it's dark back in the woods

209

glass
     by glass
 also wood

  you look out

    light
      and metal

   crossings up

     wind

       head-on

    for
      years

   the streets were lonely

    always

     some death in them

     now what

         ever there is

        so many thoughts

          to ac-
           cept

  HOTRODS

    so the same

    space

     there houses

     as the day's

     quiet

how much could they
                    flicker

        pull down

    the shades on them

        the lights burning

            night

                distance

another plane is
gas   far, a lot, the night

        shadows too

    the fish tank bubbles

                everything stand

        continue   shapes

        things more or less
    in a Yogi's dream

            voluntary

reticent

  being

  stand

    the lamp

      by the window

it's the rear face

 of the corner house

far off, the sky

        darkening

    big trees, tops wild

      space look

     direction

       some time of air

finishing

touch
  the door
   painted
    again

    shiny
    sun
     spread out

     afternoon

```
various ways
streets hold
     momentarily   each
         tinderbox   familiar

              infinite windows

         the fear of the cost of false alarms

            rays of the telegraph

           moonlight

               old south church

                   pulled through

                      the past like a fiction

                   nearby

                      the park we walked

                   cross there

                        water

                   100 years

                      there was grass
```

```
      open road

         you look in houses

            and the night sky

             any place

              is all one

               this time
```

how much the moon may be

the wind

different

places

thinking

men forms

variously

size

the thickness

like statues

out back

round earth

machines

square miles

between poles

imagine

upside down

polynesia

caves

radio track

dishes

to hear dim stars

the sky a field

sheep

horses

mines

cities everywhere

on the eyeballs

particles

                              deserts

                          streams

                      the oceans curve

                        piss, for one thing

                          to make things go

                              January 29 73   # 7 5 7

there's movies

    like two billboards

            the most beautiful

    up in the night

        towards the sky

      can't hear them

        you go and get

          a donut

                  framed in glass

                    some things drunken

            all customers visible

                  hazy weather

                    plied walls

                  known

                  often

            soft stars

              winds

                  e.g.

          modern times

          is full of

                          museums   215

curtains

shades

the ocean
          and the sky

both deep

hills

an enormous binary figure

so what

so what

a measure of vast space

the feeling of the neighborhood

while a wrecking truck goes by

and clouds

protective

coloration

a squirrel up in a tree

words dissolve

wash out

and clouds go

high   fast

overhead

216

the fog holds
        the light darts
    poured into it
                you know the excitement

        cars on the road

        the rain passes

    a quiet staircase

        pelting

        where is rain

            rubber boots

    flat sky
        going down
        to leaves

    birds river
        sounds

    what then
        moon's like

        it

            looks

        still

        the face of death

        think

            you

            numerous

            not seen

            the mind

            season to season   217

cloud lengths

specks

rain

collage

air
angle

movements

layered

speed

puff by

and time spent

windows

cavities

what kind of gas

rising

hauled

a part of the earth

galaxy

i

mean

at

moments

n a m i n g   t h e   b e a s t s

the inflection of things

begin a
mid things
the wind
          barely says

  up and down

        the house

        wall

          corners

to find

    the weight

    of things

      the fish

      the air

        support

      the flower
          in the earth
            pot

          the woods

          the floors

a cat
  stops
      there

  dirt
  the breeze

    tree shadows
      clear of sun

 cars

on the road

 far off

night turned

    look

      raise up

        the dead

        the sun comes

          the earth goes

    how many trees

    motions gathering

      imperceptible

                birds

              drive

                hungry

              settle

                tides

                  creeks stem

the faces set

    to play music

        beautiful throat

           the ungainly man

        controls

    life underground
        river

      a stretch in the sun

the sun solid
        ground   it soaks

  what bird took

      wing

    a minute ago

  now there are others

      some white stuff

    they eat and build

      farther

          there an ample world

          in which

             their sounds are quiet

muggy

 and the foghorn

   clear air

      darkening

      wherever from

        cars with red lights

          plane tails corners

            there was nothing

          buildings stand for years

            thought back on

                stars

            flash the wind

                          down the rain

                thunder cry arrives

              one minute

                          dogs

                              bark

   Out of the wind and leaves

        first rustle

      the rain straight

                  down

          the wall within

            the wall of sound

222

Palestrina from
          invisible source

               voices

                    time

               relays

                    firecrackers

                         independence

               the wind moves
                    the trees streets

piano and strings

     the wind and rain

          go together

          quite a time

               shadow

                    valley

                         thickly

                              filled up

                    lands

slow over to the

          car and

               walk on
                         forever

a car horn

   briefly

how far

   does

      the power

         failure

            go   what

                flashed
                  black

September 6 73   # 8 0 8 ' '

glad to have
these copies of things
after a while

September 13 73   # 8 1 0

the typewriter

   of a man

recently dead

   what spirits

      in our heads

   all we

      depend on

super

cool

haiku

October 21 73   # 8 1 6

h o r i z o n

an end to
        useful / knowledge

    resource

      proving impervious

    beyond supply

      limits

        any
              place

      storehouse

            sun and stars

                  moving

October 21 73   # 8 1 6 '

close

far

open

Turn it around
  the weights
  in hand

    the forces
      to come
          change shape

  the use

      of no

        thing

        lasts

      spaces

        asleep

          in dreams

        we

            make

        round

  the force

      crash of a car

    accordion

    streetlights

    dimmer than day

        they were burning all night

      stars

          it's raining

insect

  leaf

    shadows

      on the wall

        soon be icy

       accurate

       dawn returns

        in the picture frames

        reflections

          due to the wind moving

          far away   heats

           the sun so often
               as it blots trees
               lights up the panes

      gleaming bands

      around the chimney

when the twist

  of the antenna

  flickering light

   sound

      apex shadows

    trees

     steady   clouds stream

A b o x o f r r t r a c k s

crane

garage   pump

mover

shoes

a whole horse

iron

then steel

paving the way

here to there

vagueness

games

beautiful canals

in hundreds

the numbers of stars

Bridgewater

conveying goods

‡‡ The Duke of Bridgewater was the
    first to build a canal in England,
    to float coal from a mine he owned to
            market in Manchester, on barges ‡‡

chamber-pot

 oh yeh

though maybe it's still modern

        white gleaming

                call it a duck again

            shooting up

            the town

            every

            once in a while

            the law

            keeps things going

wind turned over a car and killed the driver
            how do you like that

        never heard of before a
                            few times over

they must have spent a FORTUNE

        so much smoke
                up in the air goes

                                        March 11-3 74   # 8 4 2

        such shadows of birds

            this day of Spring

            winds in March

                cross the bright wall

                                        March 18 74   # 8 4 3 '

        Fiddle

            world

                inside

                burn

                                        April 29 74   # 8 5 4

        the swings

            where the loam-pile was

            the arbor of

            pipes with

            the vine

            describe why

                imagine how

                make out cause

                                        August 26 74   # 8 8 3 b

    s u d d e n l y

        i t   g e t s   l i g h t

            a n d   d a r k   i n   t h e   s t r e e t

                now

                  here

                    too

                      elsewhere

                   what

                      next

                        clouds

                          down

                            beyond the sky

                          and one

                            gust

all there in
                              "could do everything,
        time   not very well, but
                              not badly"
        fullness   - <u>War</u> <u>and</u> <u>Peace</u>, XII

            variety

              the low man then

                Georgian hills   south

                  along centuries

                to sleep and to die

                    with day awake

                        the unthought remembering

                          stirred

                            memory   **231**

the tree-roots

disrupt the walk

more and more

up

the hill

stars thick also

some steepness

3 / 4 t i m e

put yr teeth together and see if it fits comfortably

ending the dentist

at least a while

when i take you out in the surrey a little
with the fringe on top

m a n y h o w a

country
for Clark
roadside arrow   Coolidge

to the mystery

nothing is everything

no dead-end

like trees

232
into town and out

D o r d o g n e

                             airy weights moved home

   sun

     cave

  clouds

     skies

September 5 74   # 8 8 7

     apples

           (for

    in air

            Alex

    branch

            Smith)

      wind

       taste

October 30 74   # 8 9 3

     far

      clear

           dark

          near

November 25 74   # 8 9 9

any

        f o r   B o b

place you

         a n d   B o b b i e

  come

  to clear

```
        a
                                    water
    pine
                                        plummets
      so

        tall                        rock fills


            overlooking             millions

                the                 of feet

                bay
                                        particles

                speedboat               slip

                                        earth
                man

                    lays a           lumbering

                        finger       air holds

                        on
                                            glass

                            tough        buildings

                            wood
                                            things

                            swept         mined   out

                            down
                                            lights

                            another        circles

                            is planted
```

like stores, banks

            secure skies

        disparate earth

        tight   curving

            dark moon

        all somehow by the eyes

            still known

            children

            bring

            home

            work

                to learn

                heavy busses

                the world already

                playing together

p   o   e   t   r   y

                            f o r   J a n e
        assessments
                            C r e i g h t o n
            immediacies

        one calculus

            in the world

                              (a f t e r
know how   more and more
   blooming plums   O n i t s u r a
                  cherries open
      nose and mind
                     2-legged bird

white   4-limbed beast

   to see the camelia
                        60th year
      out big
                        bending an ear

                        flowers hold

                              to the winds silence
mountains and plains, a wonder

      pain in the neck

         s l i d e

      if not

         now when for

            ever

         through the

            parts

         patterning

            eye in

            time enough

h o r i z o n s   i n   h o l l a n d

in a few miles

  how many

     birds

      winds

       thistles

      "   the unity
       of which I speak

   various temperature

   rays are a mystery

    life some of it felt and seen

       scrambling

f o r

       weights

  J a c k

      eggs in the pan are

   C o l l o m   some sign

    close the door shining

     don't take a long time

    or open it

      all the directions it turns

m a d e

uniformly

time

dashboard

parts gear

along miles

roads

gone   the curve

here and there

woods

birds and skies

the light various

through the distance covered

the stars and the seeing joined

the blind distinct worlds

the moving around thick black

in mirroring selves

‡‡ These occasioned by
Jacob Bronowski's
explaining in re
Einstein, in his
Ascent Of Man, VI,
seen on tv, that
different systems
vary to conform to
the velocity of light,
and by subsequent
recollections of
relativity theory,
 Doppler, A N
 Whitehead,
  lasers and
 Black Holes ‡‡

March 12-3 75   # # 9 1 3 c & 9 1 3 d

‡‡ Occasioned by some of
Bronowski's remarks
in <u>The</u> <u>Ascent</u> <u>Of</u> <u>Man</u>, IX,
and Victor Weisskopf's
in the brief interview
following it on PBS ‡‡

heat up and make spread fast

   manifold

 to build again
           elsewhere

  places are vague there's

    only existence

   whatever thought feeds

‡‡ Occasioned by
things Bronowski
said in his 9th
program - the one
on Bohr et al. -
about astrophysics,
as well as by
thoughts of Rbt
Duncan's work and
his concern for
the imaginative
life   ‡‡

   the mind

a clearer branching of light

 reaches out and is full

  gloom an emotion

   turns

       as much as joy

   seeing the black holes

239

sounded like

   must have been ocean

in the summer autumn
        football crowds

    in india like trees
        open and shut

   some way to be occupied

woman or man from
         the beach

    feet

      arms the

       warm air

    passing home shoes

     on steady

    to be heard

    off recently

      dried

    the trees will

           be here

             at night

   once in a while still

     you want

    another child

r u n n i n g   a r o u n d

    enough

      it may be perfect

September 12 75   # 9 4 3

the flock

    on the ground

slant

  wire

    air flickers

clouds approach

   now

  some stars
     seem close

   in the branches all
     the motion   visible

    mass

     the sea gathers

      a little further

       sound

  the glint in the water

  the corners

  you make as

   the lines straighten

                                        June 26 75   # 9 2 9 '

        what a beautiful sidewall truck

            you know enough about

                the water system

                    and sunlight

                and they go together

                    of course then

            big

                english

                    letters

                                    June 30-July 26 75   # 9 3 0 '

    Ya bingo!
     Imagination all compact
      running away like a looming train
        what would Emily Dickinson think
        the chances she can wake now   (for
    and anyway you have those who sit   Bob
     or here came more civilization   Perelman
        like SS creation and destruction
            somewhat Hindu
                        with a vengeance
            the tragic later too much
                to stand its own weight

            is there travel light and fast

            and living the life out

                                        July 31 75   # 9 3 3 c

            a run

                    earth

                ground

                    listen

242

all

    gone

        better

Whoppers   Whoppers   Whoppers!

    memory fails

      these are the days

the sound

    in its reach

    cold

      north

           is

      it ended

        now or

          something

            different

              meaning

what

to study with

  radio

in the common

  light

        why

    go to town

    if

      your earth home

      then dis

      appears

    watch out

        for the streetlamp

          listen 10

            times a day to

              the silence

              before you (can) reach

                any foreign part or

                more than one place

        my mother is Jewish

          she thinks so

the

 frosted car

   I imagine

     hearing the motor

    of the girl who lives here

      or next door

       upstairs

        now

          the snow heavy

          hours

            such days

          that's it

           news

                 what

          drives away

           the world

  Tongue-tied and

    muscle

      bound

      years

       or the seasons

         leaves

          and

          snow

resonant pile

a streak

mouth

wing

harmonica

right there

open

hands

cup

flue

times

merge

what precautions

sleep

earth shakes

tidal

foam

flats

mountain

dust

ripples

europe a map

 a moment

  on the wall
                          f o r
   chagall soaring
                            B a r r y
    self-portrait
                              W a t t e n
   has that town

   settled smoke

     from

       here

      to the world

     values

         steal

      out of sight

       how come

      the year of the dragon

          in some places

       asteroids there are

         countless

           as sand

       in hamburg

        rhenish

          at first

        sound

           complete

far away

  in the eyes

    no motion

   how much time

does anything live

   recurrence

    various

   passage

    as written

     down

      what sounds

       enter

        gradually

         from lips and

          orchestra

          R A I

          "the

            house of

             Michaelangelo

              and Bernini

               their many

                acts

                 stand out

                  from the walls

                   the music of Beethoven

                    the pope

                     sits

                      still

                       or quiet

                      an old man

all the girls
  drive around
 here's an old lady too
        I travel by vision

         vanish

      thoughts everywhere

        compass of the sun

            shade

       around and around

      you start

            seeing things

           keep on

           nebulae

          impinge

          beyond

           stars

             out
                of noplace

     as much as it may be
        a harm and

        the earthworm

         settles some room

         a development

           what gardener's
                truck
          stands free here

Out in the yard
                the kids play

    at the party Why not

        think they enjoy it   And the adults

        better for them   less serious

            now and then was

                as will be sun

                moon stars sky

            a blue cloud various

            sea   sound   lost birds

                    Whatever's wanted

                        comes to the head
                                    old-style school-desk

                    to sit with   full

                    of new missiles   fighter

                        passenger
                                    planes   The birthday boy

                gets up
                        possibilities

                    of sharp hunger, say   to bring back

                        from the garage   open

                        most of the cake   or has there been

                        more than one
                                        7 yrs old

                        "Hi Marv" yellow

                            up front with

                        cartoon duck

                            immobilized
                                        some fancy

                            confined woods

                            briefly enough

                                always

                                        someone works

                                            a noisemaker horn

                                                on his bike

                                        I B M

                                            javelins heaved

                                        with a few wings

                                        August 18 76   # 9 8 4

sun   sun some

    walls   walls

        years   white now

            now   years

                                        December 30 76   # 9 9 5

O n   t h e   v i s i o n s   a n d   l a n g u a g e   o f
          B u c k m i n s t e r   F u l l e r

              what a
              spout up

              the idea
              of

              a whale

              in the beautiful

sounds
     quiet

  down

    the streets

             range

          lost

         big

          city

        the earth taken

             corners

                 what does

                   sometime

              round   and
                       wide

              one and another

               ashes

                 fire

                  light

                    mass

         real

         imaginative

         streams

         pooled

         run

           by your side

the wood of the headboard

the wood of the closet

lean

what the place is

I've been in daily

my life

distances   names

positions
                worlds

the sky goes dark

light comes

effort

motionless

wind blows

caves

trees

strings

the sea full

parts

dimensions

ride

picture the black window

how cold can it get

    foghorn   clock

   reel   creeks

     are there any birds

    I hope the fish are swimming alive

      under the ice

February 9 77   # 1 0 0 6

so many legs to the caterpillar

   and then it flies

May 11 77   # 1 0 2 2

         for Wm
I n e r t i a   Bronk

I know too much not why
I write on these scraps.
 Ultimate convenience. A mistake.
I have begun.

May 20 77   # 1 0 2 5

    I know
     what

    I mean

    it

    sounds ok   while
    I mean it

radio
            words
  brains
               sounds

     Ives

        among treetrunks

     woods

January 20 78   # 1 0 5 7

the fleering snow

     off the eaves

     of the garage

January 26 78   # 1 0 5 9

     snow

       blinding

       cold

January 28 78   # 1 0 6 1

       bowels

         brewing

   j'ai 50 ans

```
                 Little finger suddenly
                    not so small
                         pretty far
                    fifty years old
  f o r                   its bone big anyway

  J a m e s            life to language
                         and back    and forth
  S h e r r y        there's the walk to the store
                         seen through leaves
                      the corner   fitful
                             wind   space   branches


                       snow come a week ago
                         piled up
                            empty
                               sky overhead
                                    or clouds


                     the sun shining
```

```
  people

    silent

     outdoors

        the sky clear

            day

         no wind

           distant

              how much
                      clouds

              hamburger  joint

           enough

             parking lots

              business

              food

                  the moon slight moving
```

wind huge outside since when

falling asleep alpha rhythms I suppose

how many years

without death

June 9-12 78   # 1 0 7 9

"No air stirs ..."   for LZ

music without burden

the air of heaven

so there's no vacuity there

but level steep

nothing speaks of which

on earth shadows rough

bumps lumps what's

not

mildly put

in hand

clear

day

seeing hearing touch

parking lot but

    there are words otherwise

  and here's a recording shop

     something to eat then

       dog with bone

          corners at times

    buildings sopped   by-products

     through some range of goods

         weird? is

         it mystery? enough?

      fish in the museum

      pavement mosaic

       as yet in the river too

         far off turned

       earth matter blocks brick

        your eye sighting level

      a city fixed in the ash

       likewise come by the air

         slender

          dream architecture

           opening a garden wall

           such hundreds of years suddenly

         stop pain cut fate

            as they've said

          1 time there were no roads

           (anyplace) and

           here these people are

BERKELEY

1978-1995

hills

  earth

    sky

      night

        clouds

October 16-8 78   # 1 1 0 2

DOWN ON THE BED you

    can't

      imagine

        enough

October 24 78   # 1 1 0 5

          f o r

silent

           B o b

bits

           G r e n i e r

  speeches

    thoughts

    units

October 24 78   # 1 1 0 6

o v a l t i n e

        for Rbt G.

  nice and chocolate

faces

    power   music
                               p e r f o r m   t h e
    good words
                                     9 t h
      feel how
        to do it

    h e r e

the sky

    changes

      shut the eyes

        leaves

        in motion   around

    past midnight

    in chilly streets how

      could a ball

        bounce   what

          sounds like it

calligraphy
    typewriters

  my hat

   (bureau)

    the world

     inside

      spins

the intersection

  2 levels

    out the window

      a fall still of night

      in back and ahead

        some distance
                    around,   round,   round

        as there has to be

          enough tunnel mouth

            gears

             traffic

            various climb

              lights

                the places to go

                  whatever there's been

                    in constancy

                  through the day

earth slopes and
              the sphere of the sky

     cloudy   some
                  blue

      cherry tree
        acacia

      butterfly going uphill
              toward a windy night

              people

            the half-moon already
                with its shadowy mountains
                piled dust
                        gaping seas

                    March 26 79   # 1 1 3 1

a dark wet night

          wind and rain bow

        the bush out the window

                        how
                          lights may burn

                          steady

                    April 24 79   # 1 1 3 6

       the cat

     dumb   looking

     looking   dumb

       I wonder

                move in
                  on
                a tree

June 19 79   # 1 1 5 3

    up in the morning

     ideas

June 19 79   # 1 1 5 4

    from the back
    I notice
    a harp has wings

July 26-August 1 79   # 1 1 6 3

electric shaver fanatically

  electric grazer

     wind in the tree
      up against the wall

         glass levered apartments

      clouds over the house

    after this much time getting dog-eared

December 26 79   # 1 1 8 9

    my old machine
      new like strange

through the window reflection

a plane going north

under the boat moon

everything like

time   out

walk around down the street

if

it should end ever

eternity another word

I think we're doomed
like they say

one day

how it all counts

there's a rumbling

fine

in the air   song

traffic   or the earth

a constant thing

m o r e   a n d   m o r e

days the cherry
blocks the window
sun   and   rain

sun
                grass, tree rows
 off

  hills

   mute

     steady motion

       clouds shifting

         light   change

           spaces

         plenty of time

          in the room   seeing

                 rain

             slant the

                 open air

        heat fixed in

           paving the sun

            spreads to again

      F O G

        drifting around

        cool

         parts in

          others quiet

          birds

           night settles

DISTANCE   fog

                                                            fog

       WHEELS   landing

                                                      mountain

           CHANGE   sea

                                                        cloud

                            clouds

                                                          takeoff

                        according to signs
                          getting complicated

                          to go there

                those clouds

                  and this wind

                    as we go on

                      there's one way

                        to make phonepoles

                          from coast to coast

              rock   water
                    covered with life
                                              rock
                sand
                      wet   fissure

          Heart

          remote

          fast

          through part

268
            of California

```
                  noise

                     without
                                 up near the headwaters
                        falls
                                       cloud

                                       level



     maybe it's

        counterclockwise
                                         bank the river
           all day and night
                                          the mountain cloud
              the stream flows on




                                   rock    water

                                     invisible air




                      steep
                           ness
                                                    tree
                         around
                                                 cliffs

                              cloud




                         gravity

                         feeling

                         sight

                         of

                         mountains

                         dark

                            at dusk
```

the unimaginable

power of the beast

to feel the dark

June 21-September 16 80   # 1 2 1 7

the lifespan   life   life

the wingspan   wing   wing
                                           span
the machine   machine

                                      machine

August 14-5 80   # 1 2 3 0

Lost track
    tion

    bridge girders

    overhead

    sky

      boom

      clouds

        the horizon the distance ends

Fire Dept.
  Ambulance wait

widely spaced
      buildings

  how heedless
     do you have to be

        is that
               an office
         sounding like that

           kids ah
          what kinds of bird

           propped up
           comes out

            through the red fence
            wood gate open

            hook and ladder was
               hidden and
                 pulling away

                  now

            after the van

         how much to realize

         so how is there meaning

            to all the time in the world

                        May 16 81   # 1 2 5 9

      w o r l d w i t h o u t e n d

           and the back yard

         phonepole

         branches

         sky

            transformer   271

phone

  pole

  whistle

   lengths

    track

   always

    as far

     you

     can tell

      crossings

      shadows

      roofs

      bush

      trees

May 16 81   # 1 2 6 0

t h e   f a s t   a n d   s l o w

to see the world

how old can you get

the healing taste of sleep

sounds
                                ‡ news of derailments
        great   quite a few months
                                            back ‡
            places to go

                goods

                    back and forth

                        whistles

                    and the wind blows

                    earth and sky   the stars

                        steady before dawn

                        and they disappear   again

                        no break yet

                            what a world

                        sleepy but

                    too much of one thing

                        and you're nowhere

                        the moon dead cold the sun

                                can get you, the light

                            the huge cloud dims

exercise in
  any direction
   you may get going
                 if
        hardly zigzag

          branches

          sky   area

          perspective

                around the house
                  near a tree

            more or less wonder
         always a first time
           is nothing too new

        a feeling it might continue

              getting up

            delays enough

                to be
                  awake

          the return planes busses

          at the same time as

                buildings places there
             inside having a ball

                difference between circles

spraying down still solid car

   yellow

      and it glistens

     so it's spring too now

    the street with plums

      out

       how much   time

        the bark growth will
        drive away sound

         cat in
         back and forth

         window less

          of

           a tail

          a bike under

           clouds

           rain

lightworks

   paper

work

   brake the

      body shop

        bank

        bank

          restaurant

            place

             bicycle

                 shield

          radio

             plumbing

             shelter

                electrical

                 pipes

                 cloud

                  channels

                     air

H o t D a y
         O B o y   E x p a n s i o n

      swinging the arm

276

roofs

   leveled

     skyline

      wires

     shadow

       moves

         frond

        pane

         mystery noise

          wave

         wind in

           the morning

          pipes

September 21 81   # 1 2 8 7

   e n o u g h

voluntary remark

    well, thank you anyway

  a pretty warm day

     out the window

     distributing leaflets

     blue car's driver

         behind trees

      funny how things appear

       if there's no whatever time

O   J e r u s a l e m

fighting for a waterhole is one thing

a dispute over a graveyard is

something foolish

October 27 81   # 1 2 9 4

a   c r o w d   o f

wires
  pass on the
    raindrops
      the trees through down

        might i
          as well
        come out here

          wet   bark   day for
              brahms

            substantial
              reading

              how old

            far am i going

              in the dark

          glistening some
            things let up

        movement

          to have

            birds

          besides   wind

            no chimneys on the equator?

shaking a tablecloth out front

      and loose shoes

    a street empty
                  again   while

        blue sky   some

        sun   trees

        leaves seeming a barrier

          across the walk

        roots pushing it up

          not far off

              slabs

        a little roofing turned over

            grass cracks

            umpty

        sleepy outside   I feel the cat too

          in the sunlight   licking away

            diligence   length

    the cat knows where he wants to go and
              can judge how far to fall

absolutes are nothing
              like the sky
                        an
                             illusion

     there are clouds, houses, stars

          the air's
                    wet

        streets   roofs

           hills in mist

                 branches
                           shining

          sun

            shaft

          rain

     the cat all wet

        stepping around

           the middle   distance

              enlarged

                it's raining

              over and over

Change of life? ah
    the dark rain
       against the dull trees

                Living changes   ah
                    the dark rain
                      against the dull trees

        squeaks like a dumptruck
          but it's a garbagetruck
s t r e e t
          taking things in

        the new dog

         very big

        the huge hedge in the sun

b l o c k
          watching clouds like
           a trip in the mountains
            over these hills

g a r d e n   slowly clouds
             fill that
           air
            as birds go
             close over
              shadowy
               increase
                and I turn around

                    steam

                 piss

                  fire

                     trees

                        upwards

                           the stars

                              sparks

         r   e   a   l

avid reading

I forget

         above my head

            so I talk through my hat

               nobody knows what anyone's missing

g a r a g e   d o o r s
                              for Bob
      basketball   G and P

         above

            pingpong

282

myriad streets
                a

       safe and sound

            movie theater

       foggy lights

          blur on glass

               due to rain

       long factory rooms

            the slope indoors

            traffic

               complex

                    ity

          cantilevered

               signs

               do not

               sway in the wind

                    force

            a car trailer

               smoke

                 moving abreast

        l o n g (m a c r o)

traffic passing
                    I w a s
the upper window
                    o n t o B o b
a hill slant

half in the

basement   room

sights
        lowered

gusts enough

another day

to start out

steady

rattling

I'll never get

to math off far

as the dark is here

    in   under

                                    December 11 82   # 1 3 6 3

        a time it's   w h o o p

            chalked on

        a spare tire cover

            a straight flat strip

                                    December 11 82   # 1 3 6 2

        w i n d o w   w a s h i n g

            musical glass

                                    January 25 83   # 1 3 6 7

    floor to ceiling

  big rooms

    shadows hanging and

      lamplight

          moonlight

        the street

            right onto

              3 hills   up and down

                trees too

                  long walks

                miles to feet to miles

                  around the block as well

                    the sky, chimney smoke, space

                      sleep

                      easier nights
                                                                285
                        says the second banking billboard

Henry and Rose

a couple of streets

crossing

sky and

clouds

hills

animals
when pets

grow

prominent

roaming
at will

G o i n g

sirens somewhere

and bikes in the street and

clouds overhead

occasional plane

out of San Francisco

Sunday Afternoon

the start of the bridge

big fat clock hands

how fast is time

a lot of bees

touching the road surface

junk

sound

advertisings

funny it's happened

upside down

protruded

dream

worlds

call letters a
profit clearing company

rays of the sun

2.
memory
                          time
breaks in
                          taken
time
                          to mean
views

                          it

                          a real hot star
THE CAT
                          to whom I was too close
quiet

as

a

                          always to do plenty
mouse
                          the kitten walking tall fast   287
or hardly

s u d d e n

   sight of Willie
          spending his day

    the kitten's growing up
               quickly

      I forgot

     what a place to park

       that big crane

         nothing building

      it's doing nothing

      well, where's it

      come from

     d o n ' t

      s c r a t c h

      s o

        l o u d

         a small car in the grass

            between sidewalk and street

      the sound

      of cars

      around

      the corner

      of the house

      in the middle

      of the block

      disappears

P l a c e s   i n   H a y w a r d

                                        f o r   R o n
Grutman's   S i l l i -
 Asutt   m a n   a
  Wimer's   m o s t l y
                                             f o u n d
   a barbershop   sound   nook   p i e c e

                      sandwich   ichen

                   Corrin's

        Absolut
            vodka

        Grand
         Auto

        don't walk

      Vi's
        steak

          rubber   mattress
             plant

            Tax help

    Zip
     Instant
        Printing

          Zorn

          the green sign is the thing

          there are miles and miles and blocks

     u m p h   m a n

       you prove you can

         shit

         whenever you feel like it

"I want to go home" Woke
    up or something dozed
      middle of the film there
      3 pm the
              nursing retirement place
          having plenty of space

              even without
          pictures on the walls
            where they were
            like broad high windows the
            lush big hills nearby

    as the world goes, sun, California

      and on the screen up North spread snow

      just now, wild, what air

        they were watching, Quiet they said

        huge loud

            dogs barking

N a n o o k   from the great catch

            when need there was

            that time, the feast

          we can't
            hear the narration

          what do you want a

            home is

                limited time you

            have to make it back

            before dark

                and then sleep

      Sections square Alaska H. Bay

      a boat   distance

            wiped out What's

            a significant number

              in all this room

290

          even that fly

                    is too quick for me

                         N ending starvation

                                  not eaten by a bear

                             Is there sweat in your sleep?

                         September 27-October 6 83   # 1 4 1 3

there now   h e r e
   the overlap of
     8 minutes   splitsecond
       sunshine
         off the walk
                       and an hour of
                       cloudless sky

                 a million years
                  from the center to the surface

                  gas float
                             out
                   when we can't see

                             1.3 sec.s

             the moon's

                distances

                   level

                years all

                   directions

                   the pileup of stars

                      pushed

                         away

                      pulled

                         in

                      mostly pairs

in re   complacent people
‡ My mother wrote me
  my aunt's second   mala prop
  husband, absent-
  minded, slow and   through the stratosphere
  dreamy as he looks
  and all, who went   the world cloudy, blind
  again with her up to
  Dartmouth College Chapel   weather to
  for the high holidays,
  "is a Levy," so "the Rabbi   vertical heights, miles, yes
  there always gives him an
  honor (calls him up to read   air
  frm the Pentateuch Scroll)
  which makes them very happy." ‡   understanding

                                                passes

                                              imagination

What's that cooking

cd smell it all the way in the bathtub

the light from downstairs makes the ramp ruddy

faintly like sunset

but then brighter and brighter

as darkness arrives

the beauty of

trees and sky

hopscotch

by the front steps

292

the square miles

                              (after a film,
chunks in air sound   Praise The Sea
     water reflection
and the Zuyder Zee
     gull   clothesline sails

                    climb up
                     mill steps

                         creaking around

                              wheeling

          conductor of dyke locks

          shut snug   wood cross

          belfries

     a ship steeled

                    museum   books

          old and new needed

                         air

corner spout

     season

       sky

          clock

pediment

     bike traffic

          trucks   close in
                              intaglio
                canal

                    goods touching all

real big cat

it's growing on me

a r c h i t e c t u r a l   h i s t o r y   i s

it's no surprise that
we just don't know

"the most productive agricultural county in the East"
(where the Amish and Mennonites be
- National Geographic, April '84

White Horse and Intercourse
across some lake

Bird in Hand   Paradise

Eden   Smoketown

Reamstown   Landsville

Quarryville

Safe Harbor

Goodville   Blue Ball

Bathbridge

Maytown

not far away

from Three Mile Island

we're going fast by

such big buildings

winded

dark from everywhere

lit up

in general

bushes

along the exit

path

pretty high

curved

down

many fadeouts

immediate

the past is like

and spliced in

the endless world

amid the stars

countless homes

on the way back

to ants in the sink

             the half moon

                changes the sky

                      fences

                 stood the wind

        b l a n k e t

the O lym pi c system's becoming persuasive

        i m a g i n e

             n o w

        s o v i e t   s p o r t s

    a long list of confusing yjings
            not chinese especially

    more and more people I'm trying to hear

      while the trees around the back yard
        lead you up to the blue sky

          the same air moving the clouds

        words vaporize as you try to see all through them

        m e m o r y

      the sky more open
         and clouds passing
            because of the dead
            tree there was
               in close to the eaves
               and the hours they took
                  to cut it down

down the block
  so many places

      large and small
      to come at you

    how long
      can a dumptruck be

        broad level streets
          have wide-open corners

          in the wind

        steep the trees lean

            from back yards rising

              dappled sky

      train

      going by

      bedroom

      dinette

      kitchen

        whistle

      aside from

          cars

        stop and start

          by poles

          birds and trees

          cats dogs and squirrels

walnut   walnut   loquat

love what tree

a squirrel every day

against level hills

March 6 85   # 1 5 0 4

clouds

windy

street
below the hills

a uniformed man

on the way

bound for somewhere

March 6-7 85   # 1 5 0 5

tdamping down
a volcano with
a good amount
of seawater

so iceland
is an island

geothermal
bathbubs

how many

days

firemen

from the university

of the capital

none of it
a sure thing

end History about like

   any other point

the line between
  "psychic numbing" and
   sense enough to knock you flat
               getting thinner and thinner   I think
      vanished a while back

        whatever you want in sight

                              (<u>Geographic</u>

               doesn't right now blink

            chemical dumps

      a battlefield

        night day   "... armies ..."

      Sunday

        plane

     faraway

        is peace

           a crowd

              inside

           provisioned

         veers right

      it comes closer

         faster   299

D e a t h   th is

  great

     impediment

      of all
           time

        pain exhausted

        at what moments

          building up

           one by one

          into what mass

             to equal sand and stars

May 25 85   # 1 5 1 5

    o n e   o f   t w o   n i c k e l s

     a fly walking the rim
      makes it flicker, shine

June 11 85   # 1 5 1 8

     a   b i g   o b l o n g   b o x

    a goodwill truck

     realizes space

    whatever's inside

a   l i t t l e

real oblivious bird
   taking a few drinks
 on the sidewalk
     reflecting the deep blue sky

"riding/ the clouds of his belief"

Chagall

in flight before sputnik mother kept him going though never
mind pain/ting she said baking all the bread warm as blake
keats   as 1 day he was born was the sun shining because of
man 2 or 3 centuries odd enough how much Earth might heat
 say people, cats walking the roofs the streets snowy up to
number 9 before and after the bomb till death must come your
eyes peered open for love some sharp and blurred faces

I n t i m a t i o n s

child in the drive blue
      sky blank

        ages

            12 million years in the mind
             as much as next week

         and at some point the sun
            will gulp up the whole earth

                    farther past now

thinking a
   few scraps
   fragments like
     the shadows cast on the wall
        from cars   slow
          through the street before dawn

           the way to work and
                  back

        smokes   smells

          cloud   tree   sky

                   product
                     and by-product

            something you've cared about

               went to sleep
                 and forgot about it

               whatever worth

    m o t o r c y c l i s t s !

       a dozen blocks

          roaring like that

          two by two

          planes

             crisscross

              later

              the jets up high

              bolt

              sheet

lightning

rustle

  emptiness

a car goes through

  there's a fence on the corner

    clouds moving away

      south

        streetlight

          in the sun

        4 birds

          into the tree

            others sway to the wind

          a steep wall

            above roofs

              tracks to the back

                globe of the moon

                  the cat wary along by the flue

                    sound disappears

                    down the block

          big

            big

          big

          big

            grab whole

              swallow

Your garden

a small place

on the earth

    outdoors

      however it goes

   whatever storms

      whatever is stilled

one season and another

‡ On receiving from

   James Weil his

    <u>Houses</u> <u>Roses</u> ‡

my own thoughts and visions then

  I wake up to

   moonlight like

snow in the street

    so long ago at last

f o g

  spread up

  a way

   gone

    distant

     hill

    aside

     beyond

304

     cloud

morning   dark   sea   air cover   smoke

   raining   and trees waver

clash   time goes

    sun's warmed the floor

    from infinite points in the sky   slow

     earth moving   children

      die off

     suddenly now and then

      cross streets

       without an end

        timeless

          disappear

        enough

         bits, pieces

        spreading out vast

           abundant white

March 14 86   # 1 5 5 3

     h o w

      easy to
       bite the
        tongue   in
        becoming

           space   space   space   space

                                    greener

       far from
       the back yard

          vine figtree goats   weed

                          helium

                          flung

   beyond imagination
                      so   solar
       it kills imagination

                              burst

              hydro..   water

              oxo..
                                    power
          "Dear Mr. Ahab"

                        (by now   "wind"

                        the White House
   seeing too many
                   motion

                 from the movies

          mus-ic enough   noise

               wrecking air itself

               vocal choked off as

                              by smoke

              quiet deserted

                  as the moon

              now that we know

                  (so much in

                    a juggernaut)

              the president says we must

   306
                      "God" "God" G'd?

                    what stunt man

                 luxury   necessity

         learning of good and bad

             tree walk fence

             peace   peace   and there is no

                 place like
                          (domestic)
                     tranquility

                              March 7-13 86   # 1 5 2

s u n l i t

 cloud pass

   house fast

        earth shadow

             almost moving

               street

                 beyond

                 color

                     across

                       deepening enough

                 sky change

                                                              307

old f i l m   (2 or 3 frames)

t u r n   of the century
horsedrawn Paris busses
VIVE L'AMOUR
for   crossing one another whichever
ken irby and   ways headed Sunday or not
jack foley   and these horses that
maybe died in the war

July 10 86   # 1 5 6 4

m e t a m o r p h o s i s

the cat's joints
enough known

August 3-September 3 86   # 1 5 6 5

s o u n d   h o r i z o n

a plane going on

August 14 86   # 1 5 6 6

b i g   w i n d   i n   t h e   t r e e t o p s

what shapes
moving around
the outside sound

some muscle's sore in my numb shoulder

SPinoza

    wanted to go out

       justice

      (anger   shock

        ' denounce the crowd to its face'

     but his host locked the door

       he might have been killed

        t h e   w o o d s
   repair

   shop

    home

     clapboard

       shingles

     classical

     piano

      playing

       manufacturing

       bright

C a t   r o l l

fresh fog
morning
outdoors

imagine to feel
lively in the tail

a dog so small

as to sit undisturbed

wavering sight

vanishing

verge of

like snow

increasing

through
trees

before

spring

finishing
a winter trip

‡ Schubert's
Winterreise
- the concluding
song in this
cycle is "The
Organ-Grinder" ‡

the organ-
grinder

a petrified
branch

H o m e

    m o v i e s

      colorful

    only the dog
     knows what to do

     with the chamber of commerce

      over all

       walks

        grass grown

         leaf

          hedges

           stone

          closing off street curves

            cars lifted across

             earthworm

              tube

               drawmcar

                avenue

                 square

                 busses

              weird diminishing sun   field

                  blow-up from the past

311

June 4 87   # 1 6 1 8

A p a r t y

That's the back door, yes,

the voices spread out

August 9 87   # 1 6 2 8

n o w

the moon as bright
in another spot

August 25 87   # 1 6 3 1

p o w e r h o u s e i n t h e s k y

the black hole of religion

October 1-December 21 87   # 1 6 3 3

trees

up in the air

darkness

against hills

below clouds

hours before dawn

the light

night sky

branches move over and

the wind's gone

This

house

is

a soundingboard

urinal

metallic

cars and planes

round and round

earth

    flush

        trees

     neighborhood

     stomp

      garbage

      exercise

     how can it be

      music or news

       an odd enough thing when it gets going

      a cicada

       starts up

        steep in

        bushes

313

wall

  crack

below the ceiling

    sunshine

      dirt

       graph

         steep

     up round the corner

       vertebra   section of spine
                              like

      in water around the pot

       on the porch floor outdoors

          the flagstone

                      yesterday

        past the flowers clumped in the sod

          shadow of head bed

        strange tones

          from Pergolesi

                      violin

                over radio

          jumble

           shore

            by the freeway

              and the bridge

was   will be

s h o a h

make nothing of

death to meditate on

(and life   now   green)

skulls piled along the walls

I can't believe I'm here

yes, this is the place

over here were the ovens

trees (pointing)

planted to hide the graves

at first they just burned the bodies

flame up in the sky

whoever believed

how long ?

shared space

gangland

resort

They made him sing along the river
the beautiful beautiful river
(and race with his ankle tied)
                                - he was agile
while people were dying
                    (incinerating

he had to

chose life

age 13-1/2

so he was one of the two survivors

out of 3 00,000

on shifty ground, swear

swear

swear?

s p e c t a c u l a r

i t c h i n g

maybe seconds

at a time

The rain over there
in the big tree
falling through to the ground

All my life
                        f o r

back and forth   B r i a n

                            M c I n e r n e y
across a time

scary   then   now   worrisome

wherever I'll end up

              tree

                  phonepole

                      bird

                          wire

        a rider pedalling
                straight
        hands clasped
          behind back
            the road level

          a dirigible
            as suddenly
            the first in years
              with all the other things
                the sky's wall steep
                    hardly wind or cloud

                    a squirrel through the fence
                    a green blanket
                      the back yard

          the moon's risen

              quickly

              as it seems now

I was able to
give something
back when   T o   C i d
you heartened me
as so many others
So I remember
day at
 night and
    when it returns

popovers

       bread   real   oatmeal

f o r   and apples
                   in the stove   good
  A l b e r t   for breakfast
                   near the chimney   milk

    n o w   none of that

sounds like something
   afoot

      what's that in the kitchen
         besides sunlight

April 27 90   # 1 6 8 3

shadow

motion

ceiling

streak

sky

May 16 90   # 1 6 8 4

the silence
night then moving
to day,day
into night
the sun and the stars
for   go on and on

Ben F . .   milling
round
pressure

May 8-24 90   # 1 6 8 5

a fly   free
some   time on the window
a man looking out
‡ After the film
Ecstasy (Ek-
wind and sky,   stase, 1933,
grain   Czech),
some of it ‡

a woman mends socks, space
closed off gradation

days shifting enough
at some point   hills

rolling
brilliant white cloud

a gate

swinging back
farther

to let live   319

G l u t t o n y

maybe

my taste-buds

growing young

July 26f 90   # 1 6 9 0

footwork

skateboard

middle of the street

between trees

sunlight

November 9 90   # 1 6 9 3

t h i s

d a y ' s   e y e

so it's

vegetating

flowering

all flesh

what grass is

how)   ever it is

May 20 91   # 1 6 9 7 . x

I suddenly shifted position and

really have to go

May 27 91   # 1 6 9 7 . y

N o w   a g a i n

Mountain ice
    on the rock path
    with the knockout view
                - I watch my step
                    in time

June 4 91   # 1 6 9 7 . z

morning

again

and again

morning

July 7 91   # 1 6 9 7 y2

G o o d

I've had the bagel and I've eaten it too

A mile
   mile
 square mile

   held

     air

       high

         low

           farmers'

             market

               water flowing

                 near
                     the ground

               church

                 neat
                     starchy

                       bricks

                 a third

                       chevron

                         place

                   cliff rocks

                     stones
                         clod

                     embank

                         fire

                       stars

                         up

or moon
                         over

                    game lights
                               streets

          urgent

             sense

                traffic

                 gas
                    dust

                 long long earth

                    roots
                             packed in

                    exposed out

                       causes

                          speed

                          various

                           map

                             of a cloud

                              August 7 92   # 1 7 0 5

C o i n c i d e n c e

      wrong number on

        whoever's birthday

          like enough of us

          are anonymous

            silence too though

            when you say hello

            at the other end
                                          323

t r e e s   a n d

    cloud over back of the hills

        horizon to horizon

      and fog   cloud ... trees

       blown through with the wind

          cloud over back of trees

             horizon to horizon

           and fog

            blown through with the wind

s o   y e a r s   b e e n   p a s s i n g

    the road quiet

      still often enough

        night and then day

          light up in the sky

           behind a towering tree

             shadowed   dense

b e t w e e n   l i f e   a n d   d e a t h

                no matter

                    piano

                    plane

        ‡ Last 2 words come just now, Sept 20 ,
                the other six crossed my mind
            while listening to the 2nd(?) of two
            2-hour memorial programs in re John
            Cage over KPFA
                            6:40 pm Sept 20 92 ‡

            shovel
              push

            hoe
              dice

                topsoil
                  thinned

                ways all
                      over

                  pot
                    pitch
                      standing

                        tractor   mower   plough

A m s t e r   d a m   !

Have the
real thing
    take it
 in the hotel,
the room, the
 bed to stretch out on

    the plane crashed
                    (into the building)
       Bodies, charred, buried

       deep (ly) , ground   ,   volatized

            living

            dying

            instants

                          eclectic

          m c ^{2} collaging

                        super-

                        $s_tp_ia_mc_ee$

    a g a i n   c l e a r i n g

        the sun out, shining

        after 2 or 3 days

        from a gable window

        just before evening

326   across the street

o v e r   t h e   b a y ,   t h e   b o w l ,

    clouds   rainbow

      at one point both

        and a time is there

          windy

        between storms

t h i s   i s   g o o d

    c a n d y

      t o o

what

    happens

  around the world

  endless

t a k i n g   y o u r   t i m e

  you glutton

snow

  down

   through

     trees

       coming

          again   like

                nearly enough
                times already

             if the cold
             isn't too great

                to flower

December 25 (Xmas), 27 93   # 1 7 3 7

t h e   g o o d   a n d   n o n e   t o o   g o o d

sufficient to

              the day

  Bless (attend) as
                well as you can the

          mystery

                even the common

                name for it from

                myriad time

May 4 94   # 1 7 4 0 . 2

       how many times

have I been here now

birdsong

back of the head

cloud

tree

branch

twig

leaves

street

fixtures

litter

trash

debris

a rake

forest

paper

barrels

sound

traffic

in the wind

endless   the world

turned round

so the sun

the same

variety

like all

the news

there is

to be

heard

to know

329

d e a d l y   e n o u g h

hurt   deaf

heavens   sworn

        to torture   it's

    turned out   compelled

enough ?
            a few years past

        good

    other times

            daily   good

            father   like

        on the playground

                        nearby

                    why

        remember

                    why

    how much

            compulsion

                    why

        fight the end back

                    what

        kind of life

            for young and/or old

        to have value   why

            question

                        lead skies

        ghastly trees

                    why

            seemingly endless   why

                        the torturers

                                    how much

                        is there

                                    pain -

            fulness

                        why

            cry

                out

                        what's

            any difference

                                    between us

                to see

                            why

                                ask

                        when there's time

                        if there's time

            on account of there's time

                to spare

                                in
                        our time

                        to be

‡ after seeing "Chronicle of the Warsaw
Ghetto Uprising According to Marek
Edelman" directed by Jolanta Dylewska
(Poland, 1983) ‡

slight
                          of a size
  air
                            possible

a tree
                         to live
  stirs
                       at rest
out
                          a while
  the window

                            while there's so much
soon
                                on round
  after I've
                               earth, sky
    waked up
    to start
) birds too
    the morning
                                         about as quiet
    there have
                                            as flowers I see
       been times

          d a y s / d e e d s

                    nothing shd be dead,   changed
‡ Days of
  the Dead
                      as much
  in Mexico ‡
                        as all

                            that if

                        anything's dancing

special

　moments

lots

　　of time

　sight

　　worlds, sunned

　　　dust, motes, storm, grain

　　　　(in magic

　　　　　amber

　　　　　genes
　　　　　　　　in

　　　　old bugs

　　　　provisions

　　　　　sound, feel,

　　　　　　taste, smell

c o l d   n i g h t s

　　if you sleep alone
　　you can double up

N i c e   a n d   T a s t y   M e a l s ,   s a y

　time and again they're

　　all over

All the matter of

Vive

From real wild swings to

The static

Times are the same or

Differ

Without motion

There'd be some place as cold as small

As you might think

September 8 95   # 1 7 7 5 a

To jo in sleep some day
with birdsong

        out the window

     or at night the breeze
      with stars shining
              rain, cloud

September 8 95   # 1 7 7 5 b

To go in sleep some day
with birdsong

        out the window

     or at night the breeze
      with stars shining
              rain, cloud

NOTES

In the Notes which follow, formulations such as "LE bottom-margin note in Kansas ts" and the like refer the reader to Larry Eigner typescripts in the Larry Eigner Collection maintained in the Department of Special Collections, Kenneth Spencer Research Library, University of Kansas Libraries, University of Kansas, Lawrence, KS 66045-7616. Providentially established in August 1965 through the agency of Larry's cousin Edwin Eigner (then teaching Victorian literature at KU) as a means of preserving texts which might well otherwise have been lost or destroyed by Larry's own use, the Eigner papers at Kansas are the most complete collection of original Larry Eigner writings and form the primary textual basis for this edition.

Similarly, formulations like "LE note in Stanford ts" refer to Larry Eigner typescripts in the Larry Eigner Papers (collection number M0902) housed in the Department of Special Collections, Green Library, Stanford University Libraries, Stanford, CA 94305-6004. The Stanford archive is a gathering of materials existing in the house at 2338 McGee Avenue in Berkeley upon Larry Eigner's death in February 1996, principally consisting of xeroxes of typescripts sent to Kansas over the years (but also including some later work from the 1990's, not at Kansas).

It will be readily apparent soon that these Notes only 'scratch the surface' of what comes to mind (and will come to mind, in following years), reading these poems—many future recognitions (and Questions requiring immediate Answers!), to be sure ! An attempt has been made to transcribe a good many of Larry Eigner's marginal notes (typed onto his typescripts of poems—whatever he felt he wanted to write there, for whatever reasons), thinking that this 'information' might (ought?) be usefully passed on to readers and scholars. Beyond that, a number of commentaries have been introduced, which contain 'inside information' which may not seem entirely obvious or irrelevant to readers in years to come (?). And there are (often 'insufficient'!) identifications of persons and places named.

Readers seeking publication information for the years 1952-1986 are encouraged to consult Irving P. Leif's *LARRY EIGNER: a bibliography of his works* (Metuchen, NJ: The Scarecrow Press, 1989). –RG

Notes to SWAMPSCOTT (1945-1978)

Page 3 Sonnet Published in *The Swampscotta* (Swampscott High School Quarterly), Vol. XVII, No. 4, June 1945.

Page 4 "in the blackout…" Very possibly first poem LE published in literary magazine: *Goad*, Vol. I, No. 3 (Summer 1952).

Page 7 N o i s e   G r i m a c e d Note (in unknown hand) in Stanford ts: "see FSA for Creeley's revision" suggests that this text is the result of Robert Creeley's editorial labor toward production of LE's *From The Sustaining Air* (Palma de Mallorca: The Divers Press, 1953).

Page 20 G r o u n d Text made from an unfinished Stanford draft is conjectural.

Page 25 "all these long cars…" The spelling "protuberating" in l. 15 occurs in two different LE tss (and in only published instance, *Tottel's*, No. 15 (1975)).

Page 36 g a b l e No LE ts of last 5 lines found; these were copied from poem as printed in the U. of Tampa *Poetry Review*, No. 7 (1966).

Page 43 t o   C   C LE is addressing Cid Corman, poet and editor of groundbreaking magazine *Origin*, a frequent correspondent and early supporter of LE's work.

Page 44 "Again dawn…" In 1993, while the University of California, Berkeley Art Museum was closed for interior reconstruction, at the suggestion of Lyn Hejinian, this poem was displayed in large letters around the museum's exterior walls; it had been the title poem of LE's *another time in fragments* (London: Fulcrum Press, 1967).

Page 91 "Christina's World" LE is evoking the well-known 1948 painting by American artist Andrew Wyeth (1917-2009).

Page 127 "a girder   a…" LE marginal note in Stanford ts: "The Chinese character for g o v e r n m e n t is two horizontals representing earth and sky, with a vertical—man?—binding them or putting them together."

Page 129 "the disappearance…" Holograph note (in unknown hand) on Kansas ts: "the disappearance of matter is a caption to a painting by Marilyn Perlman exhibited at Spectrum Gallery NYC Feb. 1969."

Page 130 "S. Thomas More said…" LE marginal note in Kansas ts: "Spacings and partial spacings of lines here deliberate, an attempt."

Page 148 "the mass of leaves…" LE marginal note indicates LE has been reading the celebrated long poem "*A*" by American poet Louis Zukofsky (1904-1978).

Page 150 "one little / thin…" In dedication, Daphne Marlatt (born 1942) is a Canadian poet, living in Vancouver, BC.

Page 151 "the pastorale…" This amazing poem is, in part, a response to hearing Beethoven's Sixth Symphony, of 1808 (LE looking at the winter world outside with that music in his brain, and writing).

Page 160 "intersections…" LE bottom-margin note in Kansas ts: "on reading Andrea Wyatt's THREE ROOMS."

Page 167 "spread-out…" Northern California poet and professor David Gitin, one of LE's regular correspondents; later (in early 1980's) sponsored a reading for LE and RG at Monterey Peninsula College.

Page 172 "Music is human…" LE marginal note in Stanford ts: "Debussy's La Mer on tv from Carnegie Hall…."

Page 174 "common sense…" "L N" in dedication is Wisconsin poet Lorine Niedecker (1903-1970); LE is marking her passage.

Page 174 "rain / morning…" No LE ts found; poem copied from LE's *th music variety* (Newton, MA: Roxbury Poetry Enterprises, 1976); spacing is conjectural.

Page 178 "jaggied / potential…" This poem incorporates material from poem beginning "There are many things…" on I, 74; "jaggied" is intentional.

Page 182 "Of a new   aper man…" LE marginal note in Kansas ts: "Room-mate at Mass. General [Hospital], [Boston] Globe reporter. Wm

S[hakespeare] he considered terribly difficult whenever i mentioned him. One day after an acquaintance of his, the hospital rabbi, left, i said the bible is harder, to go through e g. He said: 'Oh Shakespeare, that Anti-Semite!' I guess the most extreme example of sectarian flag-waving I've come across...." Idiosyncratic spellings apparently attempt to render reporter's Boston accent.

Page 191 "Beyond pages…" LE marginal note in Kansas ts: "Pete Seeger cited as indicative of Ocean Pollution that 2% less fish were caught, world-wide, despite improvements in technology, in 70 than in 69."

Page 195 "reflect / world…" Text in ls 10-12 differs from Kansas ts; working with RG, LE deleted "what" from before each of "sights," "sounds" and "visions."

Page 197 "driftwood…" LE bottom-margin note in Kansas ts: "At first in line 3 the verb come to mind was 'grows,' then 'rises.' This piece from a beach scene in Byron (BBC TV), on P B S just now—where Shelley's funeral rites take place."

Page 198 "Hide and seek…" In l. 25, "sandwi" is apparently intentional; LE marginal note in Kansas ts has: "...vv. 25-26 was: and there's sand / chilly...."

Page 199 "Take it…" LE marginal note in Kansas ts: "Thought of as a second title page or kind of proem for a collection tentatively for The Elizabeth Press [*ANYTHING / ON ITS SIDE*, 1974]...."

Page 200 s h a p e… LE marginal note in Kansas ts: "Not a poem, much, but thought of as a title for the batch of poems being sent James Weil from which to select a book for his Elizabeth Press."

Page 201 "zigzags outline…" LE marginal note in Kansas ts: "From reading again—C. Symes in EARTH SHIP #7—of Dada and Burroughs' collage writing from newspaper clippings etc. And the 17th because of Spring Cleaning I thought books an extension of life into far corners."

Page 204 "the mica…" LE marginal note in Kansas ts: "From reading Paul Galos and Chuey Biscochitos in Puerto Del Sol, vol. 12, #1 after

seeing a PBS documentary on power development especially in the Southwest."

Page 207 "How you / stand…" LE marginal note in Kansas ts: "See Creeley's A Quick Graph, p. 172: 'the sign that men make as, and of, themselves....'"

Page 217 "a quiet staircase…" LE marginal note in Kansas ts: "First version from a ts on back of a photo postcard '100 Boots On The Way Down' from Elinor Antin. 2nd version from a postcard to her."

Page 219 "begin a…" LE marginal note in Kansas ts: "2 or 3 vv on the wind from far-off coming to naught or something outside the house thought of Apr 12th or so in bed, but forgotten by next morning; they were unpromising."

Page 219 "to find / the weight…" LE marginal note in Kansas ts: "In an interview Anselm Hollo, citing the Provencal for to make a poem, trobar, to find, sd maybe at that it's finding things and putting them together."

Page 223 "piano and strings…" LE marginal note in Kansas ts: "This descriptive, more or less, of Johann Hummel's Rondo Brilliante on a Russian Folk Tune."

Page 230 s u d d e n l y… LE marginal note in Kansas ts: "Using this as title of a bklet I've been trying to assemble for Green Horse Press, in Stockbridge, Hampshire, U K.... Being done—word has come Sept 11."

Page 232 m a n y h o w a LE bottom-margin note in Kansas ts: "The above is an efflorescence from my absorption more or less of TOTTEL's #15, Coolidge's collection 'OF LENGTH'." Celebrated innovative American poet Clark Coolidge (born 1939) was an early, enthusiastic supporter of LE's work.

Page 233 "apples / in air…" LE marginal note in Kansas ts: "After—poem by A[lex] S[mith]."

Page 233 "any / place you…" LE marginal note in Kansas ts: "This largely from reading the Creeleys' Thirty Things [Santa Barbara: Black Sparrow, 1974]."

Page 235 p o e t r y LE marginal note in Kansas ts: "Occasioned by JC's two poems in her mag . . Sailing the Road Clear, May 1974."

Page 236 "know how…" LE marginal note in Kansas ts: "Ts from scribbling in a book, Haiku, by Harold G. Henderson."

Page 236 s l i d e LE marginal note in Kansas ts: "Or. . ts from scribbling in OLSON: The Journal Of The Charles Olson Archives, #2, p. 54. Vv. 4-8 on reading Michael McClure's "The Surge" 8 days after viewing Jacob Bronowski's third lecture in The Ascent of Man—Jan 21—hand, eye(?), brain, skill, integration I gather, control I guess, composure, sort of, comfort…."

Page 237 "the unity…" Ecologically minded Colorado poet Jack Collom (born 1931), who subsequently taught for many years at the Jack Kerouac School of Disembodied Poetics in Boulder, published LE's poems in his magazine *the*.

Page 242 "Ya bingo!…" LE marginal note in Kansas ts: "…2nd draft on a page with another piece sent Bob Perelman who puts out a mag called Hills. This piece is a response to his Braille (Ithaca House, 1975)."

Page 247 "europe a map…" Re dedication: American poet and professor Barrett Watten (born 1948) published LE's writings in his magazine, This; editor and publisher of LE's book of selected prose writings, COUNTRY / HARBOR / QUIET / ACT / AROUND (This Press, 1978).

Page 248 "far away…" LE marginal note in Kansas ts: "This on seeing a film or videotape of Missa Solemnis done in St Peter's May 1970 in honor of the pope; Paul VI and 7,000 others in the audience, Beethoven's 200th birthday and the 50th anniversary of the pope's ordination."

Page 252 "real / imaginative…" LE marginal note in Kansas ts: "Original on a postcard to Arnold Aprill responding to #1 of his mag of short short poems Bondage and Discipline."

Page 254 I n e r t i a Re dedication: American poet William Bronk (1918-1999), one of a circle of poets published by Cid Corman's *Origin* magazine in the 1950's, later published a number of books (as LE did) with James Weil's The Elizabeth Press.

Page 254 "I know / what…" LE marginal note in Kansas ts: "In re playback of my poor speech. Might be abt anyone's thoughts or words or writings anyway."

Page 256 "Little finger…" Re dedication: NYC poet and publisher James Sherry (born 1946) published LE in his magazine *Roof* in the 1970's, and later LE's *areas / lights / heights* (Roof Books, 1989; ed. Benjamin Friedlander).

Page 257 "no air stirs…" LE marginal note in Kansas ts indicates LE sent this poem to Jonathan Williams, to be published in a Louis Zukofsky memorial booklet in 1978.

Notes to BERKELEY (1978-1995)

Page 262 "faces / power..." LE is probably writing from and experiencing a performance of Beethoven's 9th Symphony.

Page 263 "calligraphy..." LE marginal note in Kansas ts: "First 2 lines might be a good title for a Collected Poems."

Page 267 F O G LE marginal note in Kansas ts: "Based on a poem by my niece in St. Louis, Naomi Eigner, 14 1/2 now, in high school or jr high."

Page 270 t h e   u n i m a g i n a b l e LE marginal note in Stanford ts: "In a book abt Egypt and Sumer I was reading abt animal wors[hip], in prehistory a seeking of contact with (and control of) 'supernatural' forces, when Mt St. Helens rose up to the stratosphere, quite a spectacular sight on the News and I figured this writer was speaking of the attempt to face the music, cope with the unseen and unknown. (Man was puny and only after the state got going did human become beautiful, it took a long while, though I think he says the anthropomorphic god came with, abt the same time as, the establishment of the State.)" The book LE was reading was Vol. I of Sigfried Giedion's *The Eternal Present* (Bollingen Series, 1964).

Page 282 g a r a g e   d o o r s Re dedication: Bob Grenier and poet and professor Bob Perelman (currently teaching in the Department of English at the University of Pennsylvania; then a graduate student at UC Berkeley) were playing ping-pong in the garage at 2338 McGee.

Page 284 l o n g... LE marginal note attests to his curiosity to 'see what he could do' in the style of RG's *SENTENCES* (Whale Cloth Press, 1978) and *Oakland* (Tuumba Press, 1980).

Page 289 P l a c e s... Re dedication: Then Bay Area poet Ron Silliman (born 1946), whose book *Tjanting* (The Figures, 1981) was filled with details taken from 'ordinary life'; edited a seminal anthology of language writing, *In The American Tree* (National Poetry Foundation, 1986), dedicated to LE; now lives in Pennsylvania and hosts a popular literary website, Silliman's Blog (ronsilliman.blogspot.com), a useful forum for information and exchange.

Page 290 "I want to go home..." This poem is, in part, a record of a visit LE made to a nursing home around the corner from 2338 McGee to watch a screening of Robert J. Flaherty's classic documentary of Inuit life, *Nanook of the North.*

Page 293 "(after a film..." LE has seen the 1961 film, "Praise The Sea," a documentary about incursions of the North Sea along the coast of Holland, produced by Herman van der Horst.

Page 301 "riding / the clouds..." LE marginal note in Stanford ts: "90-minute film 'Hommage a Chagall' [probably a film produced, directed and written by Harry Rasky?] . . . Chagall sd he's neither a pessimist nor an optimist but while he's alive just goes on looking for love."

Page 308 o l d   f i l m Re dedication: Kansas poet and professor Kenneth Irby (born 1936), one of RG's oldest and closest compatriots in the art of poetry, who made regular, periodic visits to 2338 McGee in the 1980's; his *The Intent On: Collected Poems 1962-2006* was published by North Atlantic Books in 2009. Jack Foley (born 1940) is a Berkeley poet and host of a poetry program on local FM station KPFA; longstanding close friend of LE's during the Berkeley years, who often brought LE with him to poetry events, films and other doings in the Bay Area.

Page 311 H o m e... In l. 15 of LE Kansas ts, "railcar" has been crossed out and replaced in the margin by "traulcar"; then "traulcar" has been crossed out and replaced by "drawmcar"; "drawmcar," then, it is.

Page 315 s h o a h The text of this unfinished LE poem (a meditation on Claude Lanzmann's nine-hour film *Shoah*, completed in 1985, documenting events of the Holocaust in Poland) is conjectural.

Page 316 "All my life..." Re dedication: New York City poet Brian McInerney met LE during LE's trip (with RG) to NYC to read at St. Mark's Church in March 1983 and accompanied LE in visit to the Museum of Natural History.

Page 318 *"I was able to…"* LE marginal note in Kansas ts: "Occasioned by a call for contributions to an issue of the French mag.. PLEIN CHANT on Cid Corman 'and his review Origin'."

Page 334 *"All the matter of…"* This late poem was apparently dictated, possibly to Jack Foley, by LE; our version follows the holograph in LE's Stanford papers (though spacing, punctuation, etc., are not what LE would have made of it, had he had opportunity to type it).

Page 334 *"To jo in sleep…"* The text of this late poem (given on this page in two possible interpretations) is conjectural.

INDEX

Index of Titles and First Lines

[First lines enclosed in quotation marks; titles without quotation marks]

[xiv]

[xxi]

ABOUT THE AUTHOR

Widely respected American poet **Larry Eigner**, the author of over seventy-five books and broadsides, was born "palsied from hard birth" (as he phrased it) in Lynn, Massachusetts, on August 7, 1927. With the exception of two teenage years in residence at the Massachusetts Hospital School in Canton (and summer camp and later two brief airplane trips to St. Louis and San Francisco), Eigner spent his first fifty years at home in his parents' house in Swampscott, Massachusetts (two blocks from the Atlantic Ocean), where he was cared for by his mother, Bessie, and his father, Israel. Here is where he came to do his writing (on his 1940 Royal manual typewriter, with right index finger and thumb) in a space prepared for him on the glassed-in front porch (where he could observe and contemplate everything that was going on, within the range of his seeing and hearing and imagining), basically every day.

His mother, Bessie, was the most important person in his life, his sponsor. It was she who elected to keep Larry at home, tutored him early on, and insisted he (along with his younger brothers, Richard and Joseph) get an education (he completed Swampscott High via home-tutoring with teachers coming to the house, unusual for a person in his circumstance at the time, and seven correspondence courses from the University of Chicago) and make something of himself.

All his mature life, Eigner was possessed of great energy and determination to work. In his wheelchair, from his "office" on the front porch in Swampscott, he commonly undertook to write something every day—poems, essays, stories, reviews, and many voluminous letters. He maintained a wide correspondence with his publishers and with writers all over the world (who sent him their books), often filling every inch of his typewritten letters with letters. He got his news from public radio and (later) television from Boston, had a subscription to *Scientific American*, and, for relaxation and further "improvement," liked to watch documentaries and films (e.g., Shakespearean plays and Boston Symphony concerts) on TV—all these proved sources for his poems.

Eigner's first book, *From the Sustaining Air*, was published by Robert Creeley (Majorca: The Divers Press, 1953), and the last book prepared in his lifetime, *readiness / enough / depends / on*, was published posthumously by Douglas Messerli (Copenhagen and Los Angeles: Green Integer Books, 2000). His first large collection of poems, *ON MY EYES*, was published by Jonathan Williams (Highlands, NC: Jargon Press, 1960); it was followed by *another time in fragments* (London: Fulcrum Press, 1967), and thereafter ensued a number of books issuing from his principal publishers, John Martin (Black Sparrow Press) and James Weil (The Elizabeth Press).

After the death of his father, in the summer of 1978, Eigner moved to Berkeley, California, where he lived and worked for the rest of his life at 2338 McGee Avenue in a house purchased by his then conservator, brother Richard Eigner, in the company of a household of persons (students, poets, and their children) who provided for his needs and included him in their daily lives. He became a well-known participant in the Bay Area poetry scene, giving and going to many poetry readings, getting out to many plays, movies, etc., and receiving visitors in his front room (where his accumulated typescripts were arranged in specially constructed files accessible to him under the windows).

He was the co-winner of the San Francisco State Poetry Center Award for *WATERS / PLACES / A TIME* (Santa Barbara, CA: Black Sparrow Press, 1983) as the best book of poetry published in 1983.

In 1993, a celebration of Eigner's life and work (with readings and testimonials by poets, scholars, and friends) occurred at the University of California Art Museum, contemporaneous with the display of a poem beginning "Again dawn" in large letters spaced around the exterior of the museum's façade.

Larry Eigner died peacefully of pneumonia at age sixty-eight in Berkeley on February 3, 1996, and is buried in a hillside cemetery in Richmond, California.

In 2010, Stanford University Press published *The Collected Poems of Larry Eigner* in four volumes, edited by Curtis Faville and Robert Grenier, bringing together for the first time all of the over 3,070 poems written by Eigner over a period of fifty-eight years in a format which faithfully preserves the poet's original inventions as equivalently spaced marks made on his 1940 Royal manual typewriter in the "field" (as Charles Olson named it) of the typewriter page.

ABOUT THE EDITORS

Curtis Faville has worked as a teacher, editor, publisher, bureaucrat, and—since 1998—rare book dealer. He holds degrees in English, creative writing, and landscape architecture. He has published five collections of poetry—*Stanzas for an Evening Out, Ready, Wittgenstein's Door, Metro*, and *Duration: Poems 1978–2015*—and has published books by Bill Berkson, Ted Greenwald, and Larry Eigner, among others, under the L Publications/Compass Rose Books imprint. He maintains an eclectic Internet blog, *The Compass Rose*.

Poet, essayist, editor, and drawing poem text artist **Robert Grenier**, a leading figure in the Language Writing movement, attended Harvard College and the Iowa Writers' Workshop and has taught literature and creative writing at UC Berkeley, Tufts University, Franconia College, and Mills College. He has held an Amy Lowell Travelling Scholarship and two NEA Fellowships in Creative Writing. In 2013, Grenier received a grant from the Foundation for Contemporary Arts in New York for his color drawing poems. In 1975, he edited Robert Creeley's first *Selected Poems* for Scribner's, and subsequently edited three books of poems by Larry Eigner (*Waters / Places / A Time, Windows / Walls / Yard / Ways*, and *readiness / enough / depends / on*). In 2010, Stanford University Press published *The Collected Poems of Larry Eigner*, coedited by Faville and Grenier. From 1979 to 1989, as part of a shared living arrangement in Berkeley, Grenier and Kathleen Frumkin provided for Eigner's daily needs (including him in their family), and Grenier (working with Eigner) completed the preparation of some 1,800 established texts of Eigner's poems. An archive of Grenier's work over the years, the Robert Grenier Papers, is housed in Stanford University's Green Library.